crimewatch
SOLVED

crimewatch
SOLVED

THE INSIDE STORY

HUGH MILLER

PAN BOOKS

First published 2001 by Boxtree

This edition published 2002 by Pan Books
an imprint of Pan Macmillan Ltd
Pan Macmillan, 20 New Wharf Road, London N1 9RR
Basingstoke and Oxford
Associated companies throughout the world
www.panmacmillan.com

ISBN 0 330 49203 9

By arrangement with the BBC
The BBC logo is a trademark of the British Broadcasting Corporation
and is used under licence.
BBC logo © BBC 1996
BBC book researcher Jo Reynolds

1 3 5 7 9 8 6 4 2

A CIP catalogue record for this book is available from
the British Library.

Designed and typeset by seagulls

Printed and bound in Great Britain by
Mackays of Chatham plc, Chatham, Kent

PUBLISHER'S ACKNOWLEDGEMENTS

The Publishers would like to thank Jo Reynolds, the book's *Crimewatch* researcher, for her dedication and invaluable help with the research and writing of this book.

The Publisher would also like to thank executive producer Katie Thomson, editor of BBC Crime Unit Seetha Kumar, and presenter Nick Ross. Thanks also to the Metropolitan Police, South Wales Police, Sussex Police, Devon and Cornwall Constabulary, Hampshire Constabulary and Humberside Police.

contents

foreword
BY NICK ROSS

I was never much interested in crime. I was asked to front a new appeal programme only because I was in the right place at the right time, presenting the BBC Television law series *Out of Court*. It never occurred to me that the little run of three commissioned programmes would become one of the biggest and longest-running hits of British television. I can claim no authorship of *Crimewatch* (those honours to go to its German predecessor – *Aktenzeichen Ungelöst XY*) but I soon became absorbed by it.

Actually the first programme only just managed to get on air. It was in the early 1980s, a time when strikes were common, and at the BBC scene riggers had downed tools, returning only just in time to fit a huge panel of glass to soundproof the area behind the presenters where the phone calls were to be answered. Nails were still being hammered into the set ten minutes before transmission.

So *Crimewatch* began life with virtually no rehearsal. We had no real idea whether the format would excite viewers, but there was certainly no shortage of adrenalin for those of us on the studio floor. Nor could we be sure that the appeals would generate much information, or, for that matter, any calls at all. The police were even more sceptical – only three forces had agreed to take part. Their detectives were crammed behind the glass screen in an area known as the pigpen – a description that did not go down well with the officers until it was explained, truthfully, that it was the name traditionally applied to areas into which audiences are shepherded.

I remember vividly my sense of relief when I saw that the phones were lighting up (they had flashing lamps rather than ringing tones to keep the noise down) and in the end Pieter Morpurgo, the unflappable studio director, held the first show together faultlessly. The producer, Ritchie Cogan, had been inspired in creating a programme with pace and a sharp focus, and Peter Chafer, the BBC boss who had championed the idea, had backed a winner.

Since those uncertain beginnings in 1984 *Crimewatch* has been called in to help on over 2,000 cases and viewers' calls have resulted in more than 700 arrests. (*Crimewatch* only claims a role in a conviction if the SIO, or senior investigating officer, gives the programme's viewers credit for the arrest or for finding a crucial piece of evidence.) The conviction rate has been high, and usually the crimes have been not only very serious but also those which the police found the most difficult to solve – for detectives, *Crimewatch* has often been a last resort.

But as you read this book you will see how *Crimewatch* has become an increasing part of the armoury of the police, a resource to which they can turn much as they would make use of a forensic science lab. As with forensic science it sometimes gets them nowhere, often filling in only minor details, and even when it transforms an enquiry it does so as part of a comprehensive detective process. Yet in major enquiries it has become an important part of the investigation process, and, I believe, has helped to bridge the gap between the police and the policed.

It has also earned its place in public service broadcasting through solving some of the most high profile crimes in Britain. At first I was sceptical about taking up cases which had already generated wall-to-wall publicity, but *Crimewatch* proved that it has a unique strength in dealing with such cases.

For example, one of the most dramatic investigations in recent times was launched in 1992 following the abduction of an estate agent, Stephanie Slater. She had been attacked by a man she was showing round a vacant property. He blindfolded her and held her captive, bound and gagged, in a makeshift coffin below floor level at a workshop in Newark, Nottinghamshire. A ransom was demanded and police quickly linked Stephanie's kidnap with the murder of Julie Dart, an 18 year-old who had disappeared and had then been found dead. A huge operation followed and Stephanie was eventually released, eight days after the start of her terrifying ordeal.

Although she had seen little during her captivity, she was able to describe her tormentor's car and give intriguing information about what she had heard, including gravel under the car tyres, and an occasional 'ping' noise like that of an old-fashioned cash register. *Crimewatch* would bring together all the clues – including dates, times, locations, Stephanie's own testimony, and a crucial recording of the blackmailer's voice. Each, in itself, might not be sufficient, and it would be hard for any viewer to believe a friend or relative could be so cruel, but my hope was that by combining all the pieces of the jigsaw anyone who knew the culprit could not avoid drawing the obvious conclusion.

For Stephanie herself, who watched *Crimewatch* that night, hearing her abductor speak again was a bad experience. 'His voice was all I ever knew, you see. I can remember thinking: "Come on, please, somebody know him."'

Somebody did. At eleven o'clock that night Susan Oakes returned home and settled down to watch a video of *Crimewatch*. When the recorded voice was played Mrs Oakes could scarcely believe it. It sounded just like her ex-husband, Michael Sams. She might have assumed it was mere coincidence, but she had met her ex at a funeral earlier in the week and remembered that he had been driving an orange-red Metro just like the suspect's car in our reconstruction. Her son had also seen the programme, and he too was shocked by the similarities. Susan Oakes rang the studio but the lines there were busy, so she tried the incident room number instead. She gave an officer an address where she knew Sams could be found. When the detectives reached Sam's workshop they heard gravel under the tyres and a 'ping' as the sliding doors were opened. Then they found the coffin-shaped container at the bottom of a pit, and they knew they had their man. Michael Sams was sentenced to life both for Stephanie's ordeal and for Julie's murder.

There have been other equally high profile *Crimewatch* cases solved by the programme's viewers, not least the arrest of the two boys who murdered the Liverpool toddler Jamie Bulger. Again it was a combination of clues, rather than just one (in that case a hazy video from a security camera) that prompted the crucial calls.

This book shows how unpredictable success can be. Real crime is much more interesting than detective novels. It contains twists and turns and improbable coincidences that would scarcely be credible in a work of fiction. Frequently criminals have had an overwhelming desire to give themselves up after seeing artists' impressions or photofits of themselves on the programme. One villain drove to the Television Centre, went up to the front gates and tried to offer himself for arrest to the BBC security guard. But the guard was having none of it. He knew a joker when he saw one, and he gruffly told the villain to clear off. The man did as he was told, but went straight to a police station and surrendered himself to the desk sergeant.

On occasions *Crimewatch* staff have helped to solve a crime themselves. In one very serious case, that of a serial rapist who attacked women in their homes, researchers were transferring pictures of a suspect from a closed-circuit video when they realized that the camera's clock was wrong – the owners had forgotten to correct it for British Summer Time. This meant that the man detectives had assumed to be the rapist was probably just an innocent passer-by. They spooled to the location on the tape that corresponded with the right time, and there they found a clear image of the real offender and, from another camera, pictures of his car. When the appeal was broadcast several viewers called and named the man, and he was subsequently jailed for multiple rape.

Cases of sexual abuse of children have been among the most harrowing of our appeals. Viewer response to sex crime is always immediate and frequently reveals more victims. In February 1994 the programme showed a photograph of Paul Hickson, a swimming coach who was accused of abusing teenage girls in his care between 1976 and 1991. He was already facing charges for indecent assault dating back to 1985 but had declared himself innocent, was given bail, and failed to show up for his trial. He was now being sought by the police.

Katrina Falon had been thirteen when she was a member of Hickson's elite Norwich swimming team in the 1970s; she had not been to the police before then, but she contacted the *Crimewatch* studio after her mother saw the appeal. Katrina told the police that Hickson had raped her. 'He was a monstrous, vile animal,' she said. 'He destroyed my childhood and my ability to have a normal relationship.' Through Katrina's evidence the police were able to trace four other members of the same swimming team who had also been abused. So had a university student who had made a complaint about Hickson five years before which had never been followed through. Detective Sergeant Bryan Jenkins describes the moment he arrested Paul Hickson as the most satisfying of his police career. In September 1995 Hickson was convicted of rape and indecent assault, and was sentenced to fifteen years.

Real crime is much more harrowing than fiction and presents far more dilemmas for programme-makers. We deal with victims or their families when they are badly bruised, and we are party to secrets which could undermine a successful prosecution or even teach novices the tricks of crime.

Accuracy is critical. People trust *Crimewatch* in the same way they have always trusted BBC news coverage. Even if an apparently trivial mistake is made it can easily put off a potential witness and so defeat the purpose of the programme. Thus we are usually given access to transcripts and other police records which, for security reasons, would normally be denied to the press.

No journalism I know involves more heart-searching than *Crimewatch*. We adopted a comprehensive set of ethical principles long before it became BBC orthodoxy for all producers to have guidelines. In fact the National Viewers and Listeners Association, those guardians of public morals, have presented *Crimewatch* with an award.

We maintain one overriding principle: victims and their families must be keen on our involvement before a case is taken up (I can think of only one exception, and then we had strong grounds to believe an apparently bereaved relative may have been the killer).

It is a myth that we can build audiences by making our reconstructions more frightening. Excessive fear of crime is not only bad for society, it is bad for *Crimewatch* too because if potential viewers find it too disturbing they will quickly switch channels. We go to much greater lengths than any film or TV drama to disguise techniques of crime, and we always dilute scenes of violence in a way that would make Hollywood directors wince at the lost opportunities for creating tension.

People routinely ask: is *Crimewatch* really about cutting crime or is it entertainment? The question poses a false dichotomy, for if the programme is dull and inaccessible we will have few viewers and if we have few viewers we will solve few crimes. This is no different from the tensions in every other area of journalism in which I have worked including, perhaps even at its most extreme, the news.

Crimewatch only succeeds because it has a productive relationship with its audience. Viewers need to know that it really works.

They need to believe it can be trusted, and they need to feel it is on the side of the victims.

One or two ignorant critics have suggested *Crimewatch* would be just as effective without its reconstructions. On the contrary, for the programmes to be successful as appeals they must be true to life. Sometimes that proves difficult, as when we re-staged a bank hold-up during a Scottish blizzard though the actual crime had happened in summer sunshine! (All we could do was point out the problem in the commentary.) Frequently, though, the authenticity of the reconstructions has caused problems of its own. During the reconstruction of the attack on Merlyn Nuttall in south London (see the chapter *Merlyn's Story*) our cameras were filming police, fire crews and paramedics arriving to help the 'victim' who sat looking hideously injured. The scene was so realistic that a helicopter ambulance, which happened to be flying over at the time, began circling and attempting to land. The pilot was sure there had been a serious incident down on the ground.

When a crew is out filming, people are often anxious to lend a hand, and occasionally strangers will go to great lengths to help make a *Crimewatch* scene more authentic. Once, when a reconstruction of a robbery was being filmed at Plumpton racecourse, the crew was doing all they could to make it look as if a meeting was in progress, but it was hard because the race season was over. A local trainer watched for a while, then told the director he could probably help to make the simulation more believable. In the event, he made it *entirely* believable by bringing in horses and jockeys and actually staging a race.

Perhaps it is not surprising that law-abiding people have a soft spot for *Crimewatch* and want to help, but something I had never anticipated was the reception I had when I first visited a prison. I was greeted cordially by the inmates, like an old friend, or rather like a well-known colleague, albeit one who worked for a rival firm. There was a shout of: 'Don't talk to him – he probably put you in here,' but when I looked at the prisoner who had spoken he was grinning broadly. I should not have been surprised; right from the start we had calls to *Crimewatch* from self-confessed villains, and for good reason. You could call it honour among thieves, but actually it is more than that: it is a shared sense of right and wrong. A bank robber will have no time for a paedophile and a burglar may well shop someone who is violent. I remember one call to the studio from a man who gave us a name and address saying, 'I'm no angel myself, but this was no ordinary blagging. This guy ought to be stopped.'

Actually, although you may be surprised to hear this, I have become increasingly aware that what we do on *Crimewatch*, and what police and lawyers do, is often tangential to crime, a distraction from other fundamentals. Of course it is important to catch offenders; it is also right to target a national TV appeal at the most serious crimes rather than, for example, a local burglary. But too much emphasis is on shutting the stable door after the horses have bolted, and too little attention is spent on formal crime reduction. One spin-off from *Crimewatch* has been the establishment of the Jill Dando Institute of Crime Science at University College London to try to correct this imbalance.

However, even if my years on *Crimewatch* have not left me wholly impressed by the way we deal with crime, I must say that for all the criticisms we hear of the police, they generally work diligently and honestly, and care about issues of right and wrong as passionately as any other citizens.

As you read this book you will see that while *Crimewatch* is involved in only a tiny minority of crime, and directly solves perhaps only one in six of these, its viewers have done a huge amount of good. This book also reveals the ambivalence of our society's view of crime: we deplore crime and yet it remains for us a source of great fascination.

the dj rapist

An extensive co-ordinated police enquiry called Operation Monarch
had its beginning in the early hours of August bank holiday Monday
1998 in the Leigh-on-Sea district of Southend, in Essex. Teri, fifteen,
was walking home after a night out with her friends when she was
suddenly grabbed by a man and lifted clear off the ground. He
clamped a hand over her mouth and said: 'Don't scream. Just do
what I say. I won't rape you.'

He then dragged Teri to a car park a few yards away. He made
her take off her clothes and forced her to perform repeated oral sex on
him. He then raped her twice. The ordeal lasted more than an hour.
Specimens recovered at the scene by a forensic team were sent to the
laboratory for DNA analysis. The incident was logged as a rape.

'Taking into account the age of the victim,' said an Essex Senior
Investigating Officer, 'what occurred to her… stripped of her clothing, her dignity and her innocence, and held prisoner against her will
– it was an awful offence, absolutely awful.'

The disruptive effects of the assault on Teri's personality and confidence were profound and long-lasting, some of them probably permanent. Speaking some time later she said: 'There are some days when I
just totally block it out. I don't think a day went by when I didn't think
about it. I'd get upset in school at times. My GCSE results… I could

have done so much better than I did, but I didn't because I couldn't concentrate. I just wanted to block everything out all the time. I didn't want to think about it. That was my way of coping with it.'

On Saturday 12 September at approximately 9.45 p.m., less than two weeks after the assault on Teri, sixteen-year-old Jane and her boyfriend were entering a pedestrian underpass in Southend. They were having an argument, and quite abruptly the boyfriend got annoyed and strode on ahead. Jane hurried along behind him, trying to catch up. Without a sound or any other warning, a man grabbed Jane from behind and put a hand over her mouth. He whispered urgently in her ear, telling her not to make a sound or he would kill her. But Jane had already let out a yelp, and her boyfriend heard it. He came running back and tackled the assailant, who was heavier than he was and fought back. When the boyfriend had been subdued, the man warned him not to say anything to the police about what had happened. 'If you do, I'll come back and kill you.' The couple did report the incident, however. At first the case was only assessed as being an assault; it was not believed to be an attempted rape. The boyfriend gave the police a detailed description of the man, including the clothes he wore: jeans, white trainers, and a long-sleeved T-shirt with vertical black and white stripes.

Two miles away and an hour later, Gemma, twenty-six, was walking home from work when a man grabbed her from behind and forced her along the side alley of an unoccupied house.

'Just do what I say,' he warned Gemma. 'I won't rape you, but if you try to get away from me I'll kill you with one move.'

He then forced Gemma to perform degrading acts herself, followed by repeated oral sex on him, all of it accompanied by a stream of threats to kill her if she refused or tried to get away. After he let her go, Gemma ran home to her parents and later they called the police. Gemma's description of her assailant matched the one provided by the boyfriend from the underpass assault, down to the clothes. This was an encouraging link, but there was more to come. The suspect's DNA was recovered from the neck of a bottle found at the scene of assault, and it would turn out to be a match for DNA collected from the attack on Teri on the August bank holiday.

At about 4.30 a.m. on the same night that Gemma was attacked, Yvonne was making her way home at the end of a shift. She lived with her husband in St John's Wood, North-West London.

'I worked in a casino,' she said, 'so I'd been at work all night, from nine until about half past three. I'd borrowed some rollerblades from a friend of mine, because I'd always wanted to try them, and I thought: "Now's an ideal time to try; there won't be too many people around and I can fall flat on my face without everybody seeing me." And so I thought on my way home from work: "Well, I'll just give them a try."'

She had actually taken the rollerblades to work with her, intending to glide all the way home on them, but it was a feat calling for more skill than she had developed at that point and eventually she had to take the blades off and carry them.

'I was walking along St John's Wood High Street,' she continued, 'and I heard someone kicking a bottle, right behind me. So I actually turned round at this point, because it startled me, and there was a man behind me. But at that time there were other people around, so I didn't really give it a second thought, and I just carried on. When I had walked a little way down the road I thought I'd just stop and check – it's not something I would normally do. It just occurred to me that perhaps it would be wise just to look. So I stopped and turned round and scanned the whole road to check if he was still there, if he was actually following me, and I couldn't see anybody. It was completely deserted. So I felt a bit relieved and carried on. The next thing I knew, he'd grabbed me round the neck.'

She was dragged into a garden and warned not to make a sound. Again it was a prolonged, perverse assault at the conclusion of which Yvonne was raped.

'I think there was a point where I suddenly realized what was actually going to happen,' she said. 'I decided that it would be over quicker if I just went along with everything that he said without making him angry.'

Following the assault, Yvonne estimated that the man kept talking to her for three-quarters of an hour. He told her he was sorry, he hadn't wanted to hurt her. She realized he was crying. He said how gorgeous he thought she was, how he would have pampered and idolized her if she had been his. He talked about the possibility of getting caught and sent to prison, about the length of sentence he might get and how he wouldn't be able to take it. Prison didn't deter anyway, he told her; it didn't take away the feelings.

'It'd never happen,' he said impatiently, as if interrupting himself. 'Richie's pals would never let him go inside.' He gasped. 'I just said my name!'

For a moment she thought he might not let her go, but he simply turned quiet and finally slipped away. Yvonne walked home, let herself in and sat in the bedroom near her sleeping husband, thinking over what had happened.

'I was thinking that on the one hand I was perfectly all right, I was safe, I was home, it was all over. All I had to do was have a bath, get into bed and never think about it ever again. On the other hand I thought, if I do that, yes, I'll be all right, but there'll be other women out there who won't be. From that point of view I really felt I had no choice. I had a *duty*, if you like, to report it.'

Yvonne woke her husband and told him what had happened to her. He telephoned the police. She was able to give them a good description of the attacker, and of the black and white striped shirt he wore. DNA from Yvonne's hairbrush was eventually found to be a match for that found in the Southend attacks, but even without it, it was clear the same man had been responsible for four attacks, three of them on the same night.

With this alarming link established, Essex Police merged forces with the Met in a joint enquiry called Operation Monarch. The enquiry would be led by Essex Police, under the command of Detective Chief Superintendent Lee Weavers.

'I think from the moment that we had the link to St John's Wood,' DCS Weavers said, 'the complexion of the whole case changed quite dramatically. It was evident at that stage that we were dealing with someone who was not only a person who would commit offences in a very short time, but would also travel quite extensively over really remarkably short periods of time. On that basis it became a very, very different enquiry.'

At this stage the Principal Analyst for Essex Police, Allison Bowers, was brought into the investigation. She would work with the National Crime Faculty and the Forensic Science Service to put together a comprehensive profile of the offender, and she would also search the database of Operation Catchment, which had been concluded only a few months earlier. Operation Catchment had been set up following a DNA link discovered between a case of rape in 1992 in Southwark with one committed in Brentwood, Essex, in 1998. A third rape was eventually DNA-linked; the offender was caught and was eventually given three life sentences. It was hoped that with Allison Bowers' guidance, Operation Monarch could learn from the mistakes as well as the invaluable lessons picked up by Operation Catchment. As an adjunct to this search, Allison would build a comparative case analysis. By bringing together scientific-based facts with the psychological profile of the offenders, this case was breaking new ground in its methods of investigation.

'We didn't have something relatively straightforward,' Allison said, referring to the mystery assailant in Operation Monarch. 'We had something that was quite complex, and when I started looking at the offences, identifying what were the salient factors – identifying what the benchmark was so that we could actually learn about this

chap, I realized very quickly that we had another offence very similar to this.'

It was a rape that had been committed in Brighton on 29 August,
two days before the attack on Teri in Southend. The offence had
taken place within the jurisdiction of the Sussex Police, although
there was only a few miles of coast between that attack and the one
on Teri. Allison got in touch with the Sussex force and asked them to
look carefully at the MO, or *modus operandi*, in the Brighton case to
see if perhaps it could be linked with the offences at present gathered
under the umbrella of Operation Monarch.

Meanwhile, on the night of 28 October in Whitechapel, East
London, 21-year-old Val was followed and indecently assaulted in a
darkened doorway on her way home from work. The following day
in West Hampstead, London, a 22-year-old called Edith encountered
a strange man in the communal lobby at her bedsit block. She took
him to be a new neighbour. They got into conversation; he was
smooth-talking and likable, and Edith eventually invited him to her
room. Once he was inside he assaulted her sexually and stole her
money and her mobile phone.

In an effort to know as much as possible about the rapist, Lee
Weavers had called on the help of a psychological profiler from
Rampton Hospital, a well-respected psychiatric facility in
Nottinghamshire, who had provided an impressively accurate
profile of the Operation Catchment offender. The profiler explained
that the domination and control exercised by the rapist over his
victims made him feel good. Attacks on women cancelled his recurring feelings of inadequacy, and he felt strong again, restored and
powerful. He *needed* to feel powerful. His victims were all of a similar physical type, so he was selective; his needs were specific. His
technique was to put them in fear of their lives, a situation of virtual
paralysis. As for the apparent tears of remorse the rapist had sometimes shed, they were tears for himself, not his victim, a subjective

reaction to his own mixed feelings – in attacking and dominating his victims, he simultaneously wanted them to like him. He needed to be liked. In his rapist mode, everything the man did was a reflection of his insecurity. The psychological profiler said his looks would be important to him, an important mask for who he really was. He probably had an unusual job too, because the hours of the attacks and the behaviour pattern indicated an individual who did not work to a conventional timetable. In conclusion, the profiler told Allison that the man they were looking for was almost certainly somebody they already knew about, someone who was on the files somewhere, if not as a rapist, then as something else. The profiler ended on a warning note: the attacker was upping the ante with each successive attack; his appetites were expanding alongside his boldness.

On 5 November DCS Weavers travelled up to Marylebone Police Station to meet officers of the Metropolitan Police. Their agenda was to discuss and decide upon an inter-force strategy for dealing with the three Essex attacks and the one in London. While he was still en route to London, DCS Weavers had a call from Allison Bowers. She told him that details of the Brighton rape case had come back. It had been an attack on an eighteen-year-old girl, Kate, who incidentally was just under five feet; she had been dragged into an alley where she was put through a prolonged sexual assault. There were a number of similarities between that and the other four cases, among the most striking being that the Brighton rapist had used the same threats, the same lying promise that he would not rape the victim, the very words and rhythms of speech so noticeably alike in the other cases. The link seemed certain and if a DNA match was found – test results were due in about a week – that would clinch it.

So three police forces were now involved. During the course of his meeting that day, DCS Weavers officially established a linked enquiry involving the three forces concerned: Sussex, Essex and the Metropolitan Police. The enquiry would retain the title of Operation

Monarch and would still be under the overall command of DCS Weavers, but it would also utilize the strengths of both Operation Catchment and its predecessor, Operation Lynx. The following week, at a meeting of representatives of the three forces held at Chelmsford, Allison Bowers presented detailed analyses of all five cases under investigation. Halfway through her presentation she had an urgent telephone call. It was from Ray Fyshe, the police scientific co-ordinator. He wanted to let her know that DNA from a drop of the assailant's blood, taken from the coat of the Brighton rape victim, was an exact match with the DNA from the other four cases. This clincher had been eagerly anticipated and, now that it was a reality, everyone on the enquiry knew that it was exactly what they needed and were more determined to make an arrest.

The meeting was eventually resumed and a strategy was shaped for the most efficient ways to utilize inter-force resources. Lee Weavers wanted to alert the public to the attacks on a nation-wide basis by using the major platform of *Crimewatch*. Most importantly, the matter of victim management was addressed, because in all the bustle and distraction of hunting down a villain, they must not forget that they were dealing with profoundly wounded human beings who needed support and reassurance. DC Angie Scothern was a Victim Liaison Officer involved with Operation Monarch, and she was personally moved by the victims' suffering. 'I can't think of anything worse that can happen to a woman than having to explain to somebody: "I've been raped…" I empathized with the victims, and after listening to what they've been through you can't do anything but feel for them. Their lives are ripped apart – their lives are *taken away*. I wanted them to know that I'd be there if they did need somebody.'

As the meeting drew to a close, a central fact was reiterated: they were chasing a serial rapist who was out on the streets and offending *now*, but to have a realistic chance of catching him the team needed more information; that was the blunt truth of it. It was agreed that with the correct approach a lot of useful intelligence would come from the victims. It was decided to take them through cognitive interviewing, a technique designed to strip the emotion from their traumatic memories, allowing them to view what had happened in a more dispassionate and therefore clearer light.

Following the official meeting, Allison Bowers, DCS Lee Weavers and Detective Superintendent David Bright had a brainstorming session, concentrating on the creation of a harder, clearer image of the man they wanted to catch. At the end of the session it was agreed that Detective Superintendent Bright would take responsibility for organizing the cognitive interviews, while Allison would draw up detailed comparative case analyses which all three forces in the linkup could use, in uniform and CID, across the south-east of England.

On 23 November Allison went to New Scotland Yard to compare notes with the Senior Analyst from the Criminal Intelligence Branch (SO11). Once the work began in earnest, the whole scale and focus of the enquiry began to change. As they compared and analysed material, they found that no fewer than forty unsolved cases in the Metropolitan area were potential matches for the five being investigated by Operation Monarch. By refining the comparisons through stricter criteria, they arrived at a shorter list of very closely similar cases, twelve in total. All of these had occurred *before* the Brighton attack, and they were all in the Metropolitan area. The big question was: how could the similarity of the offences, all of them either rapes or indecent assaults, have been missed? More extensive and diligent searching was called for. To avoid a clash of roles and possible duplication of effort, the two analysts decided at this meeting that Allison would do the proactive, fast, thinking-on-her-feet work, while SO11's analyst would concentrate on the slower, finer-detailed procedures. From that point, it was clear that more personnel would be needed on the enquiry.

The new information was a bombshell to the others working on Operation Monarch. Apart from anything else, the focal point of the investigation was no longer Essex; it was the Metropolitan area, since the majority of attacks now under scrutiny had taken place in London. At a meeting between the three forces on 23 November, Commander Paddy Tomkins of the Met was appointed to take over-all charge of Operation Monarch, effective from 30 November.

Monarch now became a greatly accelerated manhunt. The police now had a fuller historical profile of this man. He had sometimes attacked two and even three women in a single night, and there was powerful evidence that he was growing more reckless. The last two attacks in the London area had been two weeks before, and there was an undisguised worry that soon he might kill somebody.

On 30 November the Monarch team met at Metropolitan Area 1 Headquarters in Cannon Row, London. Their objective was to review the situation and, while they were at it, approve or revise the proposed media strategy. The meeting was chaired by Commander Paddy Tomkins, lead investigator DCS Lee Weavers, who would be acting as his deputy on the operation, and Detective Superintendent David Bright, who would now be the senior investigating officer for the Essex end of the investigation. DI Rick Turner would also be investigating officer for Yvonne's attack in St John's Wood, and Detective Superintendent Alan Ladley, Operation Monarch's senior investigat-ing officer for Sussex. Allison Bowers and DS Simon Reeves, both from Essex, were also present.

The meeting opened on public safety. 'We have to alert people without scaring them,' Commander Tomkins said. 'Their help is going to be important in identifying the assailant. Somebody knows who the party is – a wife, girlfriend, other relative, maybe a friend. While we're trying to uncover his identity, we want to be careful not to send his assaults spiralling.'

Commander Tomkins then asked DCS Weavers to outline the media strategy. *Crimewatch* would carry the main thrust of the appeal to the public, Weavers said. It was the most effective platform from which to reach a maximum number of people simultaneously. 'They'll release clips from the reconstruction to the media to mesh with our press launch on 14 December, the day before *Crimewatch* is transmitted.' Everybody felt the strategy was sound.

DS Simon Reeves then talked about what had been learned so far about the rapist. He emphasized that there was a growing belief within the investigating team that if this man was cornered he might kill – if he hadn't done that already.' His MO is built around domination and control of his victims,' Reeves said. 'Until now he appears to have talked his way through the assaults, threatening, reassuring, doing whatever it takes to get his way, and without resorting to force, but our worry is what might happen if a victim resists.' DS Reeves added that the rapist was cautious enough in his behaviour to make it likely he had been convicted of a sex crime or crimes in the past. His approach to victims and his method of attack were confident, and he knew certain things to avoid. He was forensically alert too, leaving the scenes of his crimes relatively clean. As for where the rapist lived, that was still hard to say.

All he could say was that between then and the time of the public appeal, he would carry on working towards an answer to the geography question.

Detective Superintendent Bright told the meeting that re-interviewing was in progress with the victims whose cases had just become apparent links. 'I'm arranging for 24-hour support for them,' he said. 'I've also arranged that they all have programmed mobile phones so they can get in touch with me or the liaison officer any time they want to.'

Commander Tomkins wound up the meeting by going back to the subject of the *Crimewatch* appeal. The incident rooms taking calls in response to the programme would be Belgravia, Lewes and Southend. Chelmsford HQ would also be taking calls. In closing, Commander Tomkins offered a final thought: 'Operation Monarch is a joint enquiry. Its success or failure is the responsibility of everyone here. Every extra hour of freedom the attacker enjoys is an opportunity for him to attack again. Hold the thought at the front of your minds. He's at large, and he's active.'

Allison Bowers, like the others on the investigation, was finding that the work had a depressing edge that was hard to ignore. 'Investigations of this sort are always very intense,' she said. 'All the obvious things like working very long hours under lots of pressure – everybody was like that. The nature of the offences was absolutely horrific, *really* dreadful, and everybody involved in it was living and breathing these things. I, like lots of other people at the time, I'm sure, was having difficulty sleeping, nightmares…'

Commander Paddy Tomkins found himself constantly aware of the urgency underlying the work of Operation Monarch. 'My concern always must be and was at the time: have we done everything as speedily as we possibly can, as effectively as we possibly can? Because we were conscious at the time that every day, every hour that passed, another woman was at risk because of the sheer prolific nature of the offending.'

On 11 December, the weekend before the press launch, Helen was attacked at the block of flats where she lived in Baker Street, London. 'It was just a normal journey from work,' she recalled, 'getting on the tube, then walking down to my house, which normally took about five minutes. I wasn't aware of anyone following me at all. Then I got to my front door, put the key in, opened the door and suddenly he was there. He pushed past me through the entrance. That was nothing so unusual, for there were lots of other flats and I assumed he was going to one of them.'

As she made her way home, the man grabbed her and dragged her into the shadows underneath the stairwell. There he committed a serious sexual act on her, conforming to an MO now depressingly familiar to the police.

'The moment he attacked me I was in absolute shock.' Helen felt powerless to defend herself, and in the aftermath she felt: 'Why me? What did I do wrong, what did I do to deserve it? It was turmoil, really.'

Following the assault, the man ordered Helen to give him her bank card. 'I wasn't going to let him get away with it... I gave him the wrong card number. Strangely enough, I gave him a number that was five digits rather than four, but he didn't pick up on it.'

When he had gone, Helen ran up the stairs and into her flat, where she brushed her teeth so violently that her gums bled. Afterwards, when she had reported the attack to the police, the forensic team took away her toothbrush. Later they managed to retrieve DNA other than Helen's; it turned out to be a match for the DNA already linking other cases being investigated by Operation Monarch.

Immediately after the attack on Helen, the assailant went to a nearby branch of Barclays, where he put Helen's card in the cashpoint machine and keyed in the number she had given him. Twice it failed, and when he tried the number a third time the machine snatched the card and he was captured on CCTV.

Approximately an hour later, a 36-year-old German visitor, Else, was walking on York Bridge in Regent's Park when a man leaped out of the shadows and grabbed her. He held her in an arm lock, but she resisted and fought back, landing two good blows in his groin. Startled by such a spirited resistance, the man ran off, vaulting a metal fence and cutting his hand badly in the process. Else reported the incident to the Regent's Park Police, who passed it to the Monarch team.

In response to these recent attacks, two important courses of action were taken by DI Rick Turner, who had headed the investigation into the attack in St John's Wood. First he ordered a trawl of all banks within a mile radius of the Baker Street assault, checking for CCTV images taken after the time of the attack; the second line of action was for police officers to visit all late-opening chemists within a mile radius of the Regent's Park attack, asking staff about a man answering the offender's description who might have sought medication for a cut hand.

Both tactics worked. Helen's card and a CCTV picture of the man who used it were retrieved from a branch of Barclays. The police now possessed clear photographic images of the person they were hunting – a normal-looking, rather handsome man. All that remained was to discover his name.

The attacker meanwhile made an effort to cover his trail. He put through a 999 call and told the operator he wanted to report an incident; he was immediately put through to the police. 'Hello there,' he said. 'I'm sorry to trouble you. I've just witnessed a bag snatch in London. I saw it happen. He pushed her over, grabbed her by the neck, pushed her into a bush thing, grabbed her purse and just ran. He had the purse in his hand... She screamed and as soon as he saw me he just ran... I want to remain anonymous if I can. I gave chase to the bloke, nearly caught him, I ran over a fence, I cut myself on the fence, gave chase to him, nearly caught him, but no way...' When he was asked where this had happened, he replied: 'I don't know. I think it's somewhere near Baker Street station.'

The entire call had been recorded, and in time it would be used as important evidence. Much later it was discovered that as soon as the attacker finished talking to the police, he put through a second telephone call, to a young woman he was living with. He told her she should tell her mother and father that her boyfriend was a hero. He described the attack to her from a witness' point of view and gave her a detailed account of how he had pluckily broken it up. He then spoke to the girl's mother and asked her to meet him when he got off the train – his clothes were covered in blood, and a wound on his hand needed medical attention. The woman met him as he asked, and later she put his clothes into the washing machine, effectively destroying any significant traces of DNA. She then drove him to a hospital A&E department, where his hand was stitched and he was given a course of tablets to ward off infection.

In the run-up to the press launch, Detective Superintendent David Bright was concerned that the victims, several of whom he was in regular contact, should be prepared for the possibility of taking the stand in court. 'When we caught this particular character – sooner or later we were going to get him – I needed those young ladies to be able to have confidence in me, and in the investigating team, and be able to walk into a witness box, for in every investigation you prepare for a not-guilty trial. I needed them to be strong and to have the best support, and give the evidence to a court of what had occurred to them. The victims of this particular investigation were of paramount importance.'

On Monday 14 December the police ran a very successful press launch, priming public and media for the maximum-coverage *Crimewatch* appeal the following day. By late Tuesday afternoon incident rooms were set up across the south-east, ready to receive calls in response to the appeal. Trails for the show began being screened from around midday. DCS Lee Weavers and analyst Allison Bowers were taken away from a CID Christmas lunch before they had finished. DCS Weavers was driven to the *Crimewatch* studio at White City, London, while Allison was taken to the Belgravia incident room, where she would be on hand to analyse any new information as it came in. Detective Superintendent David Bright was on duty in the Southend incident room and Alan Ladley was covering the Sussex end. Commander Paddy Tomkins of the Met was to front the *Crimewatch* appeal.

While they were discussing the finer details of the case in the *Crimewatch* studio, members of the Operation Monarch team disagreed over whether or not the CCTV photograph ought to be released as part of the appeal. DCS Weavers said no, as it was not consistant with the photofits they had already been using and could later compromise the accurate identification of the attacker by the victims. DI Turner, on the other hand, thought the picture should be used; it was potent ammunition. Commander Tomkins finally decided not to release it. 'Let's sit on it for now – if we don't get the response we want from the appeal, we can release it at the end of the week.'

At 5 p.m., while rehearsing his interview in the studio with Nick Ross, DCS Weavers was paged to call the Sussex incident room. He called them straight away, and an officer told him a man had given them details of a possible suspect by the name of Richard Anthony Baker. The informant was his brother, Kevin.

'I'd seen the photofit come up on the television,' Kevin Baker said, 'and I realized that that was my brother, Richard. The photofit was so close it couldn't have been anybody else. I knew Richard's history, and I just knew for a fact it was him. I was adamant that I was going to make the phone call to the *Crimewatch* programme and to the police. I just wanted to make sure that he was caught before he went out of the country.' Making the call could have had its consequences. Kevin Baker could have been ostracized by his family and possibly openly reviled by members of the community. 'If I could say something to Richard now it would be: "I know how close we were, and I know we had some bloody good times – we had some *really* good times – but I had to do it." Somebody had to stop him, and unfortunately it was me.'

The records were checked and the tip-off began to look promising: Richard Baker was thirty-four, and his physical description was close to the photofit and other pictures of the attacker. He had been given a six-year jail sentence for rape in 1987, and in 1995 he was sentenced to four years for having unlawful sex with a fifteen-year-old girl. Alan Ladley called Lee Weavers and told him of this tip-off, and Lee felt that Baker was one of the most promising suspects they had so far.

'When I heard that the call had come into the Sussex incident room I immediately felt a degree of elation and a degree of hope,' said Commander Tomkins. But he was a man with a lot of police experience, so he was cautious too. 'There was clearly some good information there for us to explore, but I was also very much aware that *Crimewatch* was the culmination of our press strategy, and that we couldn't afford to miss the opportunity it gave us to get a clear and comprehensive message across to the biggest possible audience.'

A serious problem loomed. Major resources had already been put into the south-east – including London – to be ready if the opportunity for an arrest should arrive. According to his brother, Richard Baker was at that time living in the family home at Bodmin, Cornwall; worse than that, he was due very soon to leave for Spain.

A makeshift incident room was set up alongside the *Crimewatch* studio and Lee was there to co-ordinate and ensure immediate reaction to calls coming in. Allison Bowers was at the Belgravia incident room ready to run the new details through the Suspect Matrix, which would test the probability that Richard Baker was the man they were chasing. After looking at the results, Allison was impressed with the strength of the evidence.

'There were strong issues around how we intercepted our suspect,' said Commander Tomkins: 'what course of action we would have to take in terms of an arrest, the reasons for our arrest, what impact that would have on the other cases we were investigating, and what our strategy would be beyond the point of arrest.'

On a three-way conference call with DCS Weavers and DI Turner, Detective Superintendent Bright, who had been dealing with the victims at first hand, began to lose his temper over the reluctance to make an arrest, especially when he heard that the suspect would soon be travelling to Torremolinos, Spain, where he worked as a DJ. 'If he's the man we're after, and if he gets away, it will take years to haul him back, and in the meantime there'll be

Lord knows how many other victims.' After a few more heated exchanges, a decision was made to effect the arrest of Richard Baker.

It was now almost 8 p.m. It was also ten days away from Christmas. After serious but unsuccessful attempts to get hold of a helicopter or hire some other aircraft to fly officers to Bodmin to arrest Baker, a team from Sussex and another from the Met were dispatched to Cornwall. Meanwhile, the one and only officer on duty at Bodmin CID was ordered to round up a couple of constables for backup, then go and keep an eye on the Bakers' family home. It was always possible that Baker would start moving after the *Crimewatch* appeal had been transmitted, so Bodmin's orders were to watch and wait. If Baker should leave the house, they were to arrest him.

When the appeal was screened, Nick Ross opened by telling viewers that one of the biggest police enquiries ever was now under way, involving three forces headed by a commander in the Met. Dozens of offences committed in recent years were being reviewed, and, so far at least, ten had been positively linked. In spite of varying descriptions, it was now highly possible that one man had been responsible for a large number of stranger rapes in London and the south of England. Later in the programme, as Nick interviewed Commander Tomkins, he said that the attacks had been so prolific that there could be dozens of women who had been attacked by the same man and hadn't told the police.

'That's right,' the commander said. 'I would urge any woman who feels that she may have been a victim of this man to come forward.'

The response was good. Women did come forward. Information was being steadily processed in the makeshift incident room in the studio. DCS Weavers received a fax telling him that earlier that year Richard Baker had been charged with rape and indecent assault in Spain, but the charges had been dropped. This, for Lee, was it – he was convinced that this was their man.

Elsewhere, the picture was not so promising. In Bodmin, it was unfortunate that due to the open aspect of the Baker family house, the stake-out police had been obliged to park some way off to avoid being spotted. When a car rolled out of the Bakers' driveway a short time after the *Crimewatch* appeal ended it left unnoticed. Once this was discovered some frantic checking around was done and Kevin Baker was contacted for assistance. He was eventually able to tell the police that his brother had caught a late bus from Lostwithiel and was heading for Heathrow.

The police were running out of time. They now knew that Baker was on the night coach and that he had to transfer to another coach at Heathrow, at around 6 a.m., that would go to Gatwick, where Baker was booked on an early flight to Spain. Two officers from the Belgravia incident room travelled to Heathrow with orders to inter-cept Baker and arrest him. Neither officer knew what Baker really looked like; they had only a basic description and the photofits to go on. Both men were extremely tired, and at that hour, in the run-up to Christmas, Heathrow was packed with travellers.

The officers eventually located the bay where the Lostwithiel coach was scheduled to arrive and found it was already there. It appeared to be empty. Then a man with a bandage on his hand got off, and the officers realized how good the photofits were. They went up to him and identified themselves, and one of them asked the man if he was Richard Baker. He said he was, and they arrested him.

From Heathrow he was taken to Belgravia, where he appeared in court on a holding charge and was given a three-day detention. In the meantime, his three kitbags had been searched. Officers found a black and white striped, long-sleeved T-shirt and a bottle of tablets with a label from a Basildon hospital pharmacy, which placed Baker in the south-east region on the day of the last two attacks. They also found his address book.

In Bodmin, a search at Baker's mother's house turned up a calendar charting his trips to Spain. Police in Torremolinos confirmed that Richard Anthony Baker had recently been arrested for drugging and sexually assaulting a young girl, and was suspected of other offences. The drug used was Rohypnol (flunitrazepam), known as the date-rape drug because of its capacity, especially in combination with alcohol, to make a user pass out very rapidly. A quantity of the drug was subsequently found among his possessions, together with Polaroid photographs of some of his victims.

On Baker's return to Belgravia Police Station, Detective Superintendent Bright and a full interview team were waiting for him. Three days of questioning began. In spite of breaking down in tears several times during interviews, Baker maintained a line of 'no comment'.

'I can remember being told, "We've got him, he's in",' said DC Angie Scothern, Victim Liaison Officer. 'And you want to tell people, you want to tell the victims: "We've got this person in custody that we believe has attacked you." But then you always get the question: "How do you know it's him?"'

When the DNA results came back from the lab, the police knew for sure they had the right man: Baker's DNA showed a one-in-ten-million match with the DNA of the attacker.

'I was just amazed,' said Yvonne, victim of the assault in St John's Wood. 'You always wonder whether he's going to be found. He might walk around for ever. And to actually hear they'd found him was brilliant. It was just amazing – it was a very good Christmas present.'

Between sessions of questioning, ID parades were set up, and Baker was positively identified by three victims. As a result of this, the DNA evidence and fingerprint evidence, he was charged with three more attacks.

At his trial at the Old Bailey during May and June 1999, Baker pleaded guilty to indecent assaults on Gemma and Tina – fingerprint evidence had been found in both cases. He also pleaded guilty to indecent assault on Helen; a cashpoint photograph put him at a bank with her card. He entered a guilty plea to a charge of assault occasioning actual bodily harm against Else – the police recording of his voice was held to be very strong evidence in this case. He pleaded not guilty to a number of other charges of rape and indecent assault, thereby obliging the victims to go through the ordeal of public cross-examination.

'Seven of his victims had to give evidence in court,' said Detective Superintendent Bright. 'That is an ordeal in its own right, to give evidence in a court that is absolutely bursting with people when you take into account the press, families of victims, supporters of Baker and members of the public. Those victims had to go into the witness box and relive their very worst nightmare.'

'At first I was so wrapped up with actually getting there without falling over, and sitting down and answering questions and stuff, that I'd forgotten he was even there,' said one of the victims. 'Then suddenly there was a pause in the questioning, and I looked over, and I was really, really surprised. I'd thought I would recognize him instantly. I thought there would be no doubt in my mind at all, and when I saw him it wasn't like that at all. He just looked perfectly ordinary, like anybody you could meet in the street.'

Another victim said: 'When I first saw this person I had never seen before, who had damaged me, there was just this feeling of total hatred. He was just a sad, lonely man there. He appeared just... normal.'

During cross-examination Baker said: 'I just wanted to be totally, totally in control. In all the attacks, I tried to terrorize my victims, tried to put so much fear in them.'

His diaries and address books revealed that during the most active period of his attacks, Baker had visited several girlfriends in the south-east of the country, all of them women he had first met in Spain. Neither the girlfriends nor their families realized that Baker was using their homes as bases of operation. When he was not with them, he was out tracking down women to attack.

'What makes someone like Baker what he is, behave the way he has, I don't know – it's a mixture of nature and nurture,' said Commander Paddy Tomkins. 'But he has exercised a choice in attacking the women in the way he did. He exercised a choice when he forced victims to give evidence in court. He will always be in a position to exercise a choice. The responsibility must be his.'

On 16 June 1999 Richard Baker was given four life sentences. He will be eligible to apply for parole in 2011. However, this does not mean that he will automatically be successful because of the seriousness of his crime. The police continued to investigate many cases over the following months before the investigation was concluded.

Among the issues raised by this case was the vexed question of the charge of indecent assault, which currently carries less weight, both in the way it is perceived and in how it is punished, than the charge of rape. Looking at Richard Baker's offences, it is hard for many people to believe that so much misery and torture, classified by the law as indecent assault, could have been any less of an ordeal than rape. Detective Superintendent Alan Ladely of Sussex Police is on the Review Board of Sexual Offences at the Home Office and is working for reform in this area.

Throughout the long trial at the Old Bailey there was recurring comment among the media and the public on how ordinary and inoffensive Richard Baker looked. It was almost as if people felt cheated: evil without an evil face was unfair.

'I was struck by Baker's ordinariness when I first saw him in the cell block,' said Commander Paddy Tomkins. 'I think the lesson for all of us is that there are no monsters. There are only ordinary people who do monstrous things.'

the handcuff
robber

The investigation called Operation Diamond was set up by Hampshire Constabulary in February 1998 in response to an armed robbery at the premises of a travel agent in Southampton. In the course of the robbery, which was carried out by one man, sixteen members of the agent's staff were handcuffed at gunpoint before the robber made off with a substantial amount in currency and traveller's cheques.

Within an hour of the robbery being committed, the travel agent's branch security came to the premises and spoke with the officer in charge of the investigation, Detective Inspector Nigel Niven. They told him they suspected that the robber was Ian Bernard Phelps, thirty-four, a man they believed had been committing handcuff robberies at branches of the travel agent since 1994. His first one, they suspected, had been in March of that year at the company's Brighton premises. Phelps was arrested for that robbery, but because there was a major lack of evidence he was released without charge. Since that time, whenever there was an armed robbery where handcuffs were used to restrain staff, Phelps was considered a prime suspect. He had been arrested a number of times, but for various reasons he had not been successfully prosecuted.

DI Niven listened closely to what the agent security staff had to say. 'Like any investigating officer,' said DI Niven, 'I am expected to keep an open mind. However Phelps did seem like a very good potential suspect. Having said that, suspecting something and proving it in a court of law are two very different things.'

It was at this point that DI Niven formed Operation Diamond. Initially the team was large but, as time went by, it was condensed to a small core team of detectives led by DI Niven. The principle members were Detective Sergeant (now Detective Inspector) Dave Dilly and Detective Constable Ron Ash. 'Having seen the absolute distress and trauma caused to the staff at the scene,' said DI Niven, 'I decided that the man behind these crimes had to be caught – be it Phelps or whoever.'

Following the Southampton robbery in February 1998, enquiries established that Phelps had been living in the town at the time. At the end of March he was arrested and questioned. He steadfastly denied any connection with the crime; when invited to take part in an identification parade, he refused. A covert video was made, however, and Phelps was subsequently identified by two members of the cleaning staff at the Southampton travel agent. Phelps was charged with the robbery.

'We actually charged him at that time,' said DI Dave Dilly. 'But having taken advice from counsel, we basically decided that the evidence we had, although not flimsy, wasn't the strongest case.'

The main problem was that there was no forensic evidence linking Phelps to the robbery. He is the kind of criminal who nowadays is described as being forensically aware, and he usually left few traces of his presence at the scene of a crime.

'At that time there were a number of lines of enquiry which we were pursuing,' DI Dilly said, 'and by having him charged we were basically putting ourselves under pressure against the clock. So having spoken to counsel, we discontinued the charges at that time, but made him aware that we were still carrying out further enquiries – in fact, we put that in writing to his solicitors.'

DI Nigel Niven explained that the point of dropping the charges against Phelps was to gain the time to put together a stronger case. 'We had a pretty good case, but we felt it wasn't enough and what we knew was that if we widened our enquiry and re-investigated all the offences that had been committed elsewhere, outside Hampshire, we would be able to develop a case which would involve a lot of "similar fact" evidence.'

The operating principle of so-called similar fact evidence is that if several outstanding features of several crimes are closely similar, then it can be persuasively asserted that only one person could have committed those crimes. A phrase used by Operation Diamond barristers is 'whoever committed one robbery, committed all'.

The enquiry strategy for Operation Diamond was three-pronged: to re-investigate all the robberies Phelps was suspected of committing, to conduct a full financial investigation of him, and to find out how all the stolen traveller's cheques and travel vouchers had been used, with a view to linking Phelps to receivers of stolen property.

Phelps was suspected of committing fifteen major robberies in just over five years – six of which were at travel agents. Subsequently, when he was on the run from Operation Diamond officers, he committed robberies at betting shops in Sussex, Wiltshire, Avon and Somerset. He never robbed the same branch more than once. In all but two of the robberies he operated alone; in a robbery at a travel agent in Canterbury on 14 February 1995, and another on the following day at a betting shop in Southampton, two men carried out the theft.

Because Phelps took care to leave minimal traces of himself at the scene of a robbery, there was very little cumulative forensic evidence linking him to the crimes, and certainly not enough to make a credible case.

'So our case was based quite substantially on the similar fact evidence: in effect, circumstantial evidence,' said Detective Inspector Niven. 'Now, in policing terms, circumstantial evidence isn't often regarded as being strong evidence. But the reality is that, when put together, it can build an insurmountable case.'

Careful study of the records of the robberies produced eight instances of similar fact evidence: the use of handcuffs; the robber's Scottish/Northern Irish accent; use of the phrase 'Don't look at my face'; he always locked the front door; he always promised a welfare call (that is, when leaving the scene he would promise to call an emergency service so that the handcuffed staff would soon be set free); the robberies were always committed at the same time of day; the robber always carried a handgun; the getaway was always in a taxi.

'It was quite largely circumstantial evidence,' said DI Dilly, 'but in some offences there was a lot of additional evidence. For example, we looked at his financial spending patterns over six years, and we identified a number of bank accounts or building society accounts that he was using.'

Simple analysis showed that when Phelps had no money, robberies were committed. Shortly after each robbery, substantial sums of money appeared in his accounts.

'We were able to analyse cashpoint usage, and so we could show that he was in the relevant towns at the relevant times. Probably the most obvious example was on the day of a robbery that was committed in Bath. Virtually the identical sum that was stolen during the robbery he deposited in a building society account.'

Robbers are often successfully identified from CCTV footage, but in the fifteen robberies under scrutiny by Operation Diamond the available video was no help in identifying the thief because he always wore a disguise. In the earlier robberies, some of the props, such as joke-shop beards, were outlandish and not even intended to pass for normal, but later he became quite subtle and seemed to understand that a few artful touches can substantially alter a person's appearance.

In the Southampton robbery, it was believed that he had done no more than stick on a pair of false sideburns. It was apparent, too, that he came to realize that prominent features stick in the mind of a witness, and probably to that end Phelps spent part of the proceeds of a robbery on having his batwing ears surgically pinned back.

'On a previous occasion as well,' said DI Niven, 'he used the proceeds of a robbery to get his somewhat rotten, decayed teeth replaced, so perhaps he was thinking to the future.'

One identifying feature that was not so easily corrected was a tattoo of a caterpillar on the lobe of Phelps' left ear. When being questioned, he had often said in his defence that people would have been able to identify him easily from that tattoo. Later it would be discovered that when he was committing robberies he would cover the tattoo with sticking plaster or make-up, depending on his whim. Eventually, CCTV evidence came to hand which revealed a light-coloured mark on the robber's left ear, identifying not his tattoo but his attempt to disguise it.

When the enquiry team had reached the point where they were satisfied that they had put together a strong enough case to take to court, they were faced with the problem of finding Ian Phelps, who had gone missing since the charges against him in the Southampton robbery had been dropped. He had a rented-accommodation address in Bath, but efforts to arrest him there failed.

'He'd basically gone on the run,' said DI Niven. 'We knew then that the best way of getting hold of him was to enlist the public's support, and that's why we went to *Crimewatch*.'

The slot on *Crimewatch* was scheduled for 13 July. During rehearsal on the day of the programme, Phelps committed an armed robbery on the premises of a travel agent in Worcester. DI Dilly and DC Ash were in the *Crimewatch* studio at the time, and when they heard the news they had no doubt that the robber was Phelps, the subject of their upcoming appeal that day.

'It was the time of day – he went in at exactly the right time.

There was a gun produced, staff were asked to lock the doors, they were handcuffed...' A classic Phelps robbery, in fact, and there had even been the promise of a welfare call. The Operation Diamond team actually co-ordinated the chase from the studio. Because they knew Phelps' pattern of behaviour, they were able to anticipate his moves. The getaway would be in a taxi, and it would either be a trip to the railway station or a long taxi journey to another town. Worcester police were told they should stake out the railway station and those in the surrounding districts; they should also get in touch with all the nearby taxi firms and warn them to look out for a man fitting Phelps' description. Before very long, word came back from Worcester that Phelps was already on his way to Gloucester in a taxi.

'We lost the trail there,' said DI Dilly, 'but it was an ongoing live incident where there was half a chance that at one point we might actually get him before the programme went out, even though this would have left a gap to fill in the programme. The priority, of course, for both the police and the *Crimewatch* team, was that the villain be caught.

When the appeal was broadcast, Phelps' photograph was shown and viewers were asked to call if they had seen him recently, or if they had information about where he was living. Around forty calls were made in response to the appeal, and they were all followed up, but none of them led the police to Phelps.

Before the television appeal there had been a string of six robberies at roughly weekly intervals, all bearing Phelps' hallmark. With the Worcester robbery on the day of the appeal, the robberies stopped.

'Well, basically, what we believe happened is that following *Crimewatch* he was actually made aware that he'd been on the programme, and we believe that from that point on he changed his identity, and we subsequently found out that within three or four days of *Crimewatch* going out he was living in Edinburgh under a false identity with ginger hair!'

But for six weeks after the appeal the police still had no idea where

Phelps was. Behind the scenes the Operation Diamond team worked hard to trace his whereabouts. Their efforts were rewarded in early September when they discovered Phelps' mobile telephone number. Like a number of criminals, Phelps engaged in the practice of buying 'pay as you go' phones and replacing them after a short period of time. Although Phelps was no longer in possession of the phone, the police managed to use it to identify a woman in Inverness. When police interviewed her, she told them that Phelps was living in Edinburgh. She didn't know his home address, but he regularly used a café in the Leith Walk area. A surveillance team was set up to watch the café, and towards the end of the second day Phelps appeared. He was arrested by DI Dilly and DC Ash and flown to Southampton for questioning.

Throughout his interrogation Phelps refused to answer any questions relating to the robberies, and he wouldn't tell the police where he had been living in Edinburgh. As soon as he had been charged with thirteen counts of armed robbery, Niven, Dilly and Ash flew back to Edinburgh, taking with them a set of keys Phelps had on him at the time he was arrested.

'It was a bit like Cinderella and the slipper,' said DI Dilly. 'We had the keys, and we just had to find the door that they fitted.'

A half-page appeal was printed in the *Scotsman* which included a photograph of Phelps and the keys. Meanwhile, DI Niven and DI Dilly went to Inverness to speak to Phelps' former girlfriend. She told them that Phelps had visited her there once and that they had stayed at a guesthouse. The detectives then went to the guesthouse in question and asked to see the register. The register had no entry in Phelps' name. However, they noticed an entry on 10 August in the name of Lee Martin. They knew this to be the name of an associate of Phelps and suspected that he may have been using it to cover his identity. The entry also gave an address – 25 Montemery Street, Edinburgh. There is no such street in the city, but the detectives knew that close to where Phelps was arrested there was a Montgomery Street.

Immediate contact was made with CID officers from Edinburgh who went to the adddress while DI Niven and DI Dilly waited for the outcome to their enquiry. The keys didn't fit any of the doors at number 25. The officers tried them in other doors at houses along the street, and five doors to the left of 25, at number 15, the keys fitted the lock of flat number 1. The landlord confirmed that he had let the bedsit to a man calling himself Lee Martin. Having established that they had found Phelps' hideaway, the Scottish officers went before the local sheriffs and applied for a warrant to search the bedsit on Montgomery Street. In the meantime, DI Niven and DI Dilly were heading south from Inverness, carefully planning en route their next crucial moves.

DI Niven explained the thoroughness he wanted in the search of the room. 'We were going to treat it as a crime scene and examine it as we would a murder scene. We were very keen to support our already strong case with some good forensic evidence, and we were hopeful – I can put it no higher than that – we were hopeful of finding some evidence within the flat. Well, as events turned out, we found some tremendous evidence within that room.'

Dilly agreed. 'It was like hitting the jackpot. We found his full robber's kit.'

There was a black handgun, exactly as described many times by witnesses; a black rucksack with blue stripes, just as described by witnesses at Phelps' last robbery in Worcester; seven pairs of handcuffs; a partially used packet of surgical gloves, the kind he always wore on robberies; a make-up stick, matching the cosmetic cover-up he wore on his ear when he was arrested.

'So we had this additional evidence,' said Niven, 'but what struck us both at the time was that it was crucial that we got Phelps, because that kit was ready to go. I'm absolutely convinced that he was about to do another robbery, and, having seen the misery he'd caused on the previous robberies, it was a great relief to have him *and* his kit.'

The impact of any robbery on the people involved can be traumatic in the extreme, but armed robbery coupled with physical restraint can have catastrophic long-term effects. Talking of Phelps' victims, Niven said: 'To some people who were robbed it was totally devastating. They had to leave their jobs, they can't work – it was to a varying degree... But some of the victims had just lost all their confidence, they're constantly looking at the door where they're working. A number of them have actually given up jobs where they come into contact with the public.'

During the trial of Ian Phelps, there was only one point at which the police feared that he would not be convicted. Niven explained: 'There came a stage in the court case when I was so glad we put the matter out on *Crimewatch*. At a very late stage, Ian Phelps introduced evidence to suggest that he had had a black eye during the course of a number of the later robberies. Now, our witnesses had made no reference to the robber having a black eye. Our case was based significantly on similar fact evidence: that is, whoever had done one of those robberies had done them all. If Phelps was able to satisfy the jury that he had had a black eye – and therefore he couldn't have been that robber – then there was a serious risk that *all* the charges may be put in peril.'

Fortunately, one of the callers to *Crimewatch* following the Phelps appeal was a person who had known Phelps throughout the relevant period. This witness attended the trial at very short notice and gave evidence that Phelps did not have a black eye at that time, and the court accepted the statement as being truthful.

Ian Phelps was found guilty of armed robbery on eleven counts and was sentenced to fourteen years' imprisonment, of which he is expected to serve a minimum of nine years.

DI Niven said: 'I've been a detective for many years, my primary task to investigate murder. They are very satisfying cases in which to convict, but I have to say that this case was special. When Phelps was convicted, the atmosphere in the court was electric, and I've never experienced that before.'

DI Dilly admitted there was a great feeling of job satisfaction. 'And to have one of the victims actually come up and say thank you – that was tremendous. Made the hair stand up on the back of my neck.'

murder
without
motive

In the investigation of crime it is always important for the police to establish a motive, but in 1995, in the East Riding of Yorkshire, in the village of Burton Fleming, there was a murder which appeared to have no motive at all.

It happened on 9 February, a cold day that began as usual for the Wilsons when Ted, a farmer, left the house at 7.30 a.m. to go to work. An hour later his wife, Margaret, went to the local shop; on the way back she took a newspaper to her neighbour, Mrs Sutton, and stayed a few minutes to talk. She then went home and spent the rest of the morning baking. At noon Ted came back for his lunch. Their son, Alan, arrived at about one o'clock to do a few odd jobs at the house. He went back to the farm with his father at 1.30 p.m. It could not have been a more humdrum, ordinary day.

A little after two o'clock Margaret's daughter Heather came to visit. They had tea, then around 3:15 p.m. Heather gave her mother a lift part of the way along the road from Burton Fleming to Rudston, the idea being that Margaret could have a brisk walk back home, something she liked to do. Shortly after 3:20 p.m. two farm workers, David Tilsley and Robert Blake, working on a farm opposite Ted Wilson's, saw Margaret walking along the road in the direction of Burton Fleming. A minute or so later Tilsley noticed a white Montego estate car parked on the grass verge, facing Rudston. A man was walking away from the car in the same direction as Margaret. As Tilsley watched, the man broke into a run. Tilsley called Robert Blake on his CB radio and said it looked as if the man was chasing Margaret. When the man reached Margaret he seemed, in Tilsley's words, to 'lurch over her', and then they both disappeared from view behind the hedge. Later, Blake's account of the sequence of events would match Tilsley's, except that he believed the Montego could have been either silver or white. Both men said that as the stranger reached Margaret Wilson, she still didn't appear to know he was there.

Tilsley and Blake were at least four hundred yards away when the attack happened. As they ran across the field, they saw the man go back to his car. He was running and then leaped into the car and drove off south towards Rudston. When Tilsley and Blake reached the road, they walked along the verge and found Margaret lying face down on the grass. They could both see she had a large, ugly wound on her neck, and blood had seeped on to the grass around her head. There was no sign of life. Tilsley flagged down a motorist and asked him to raise the alarm. A few minutes later, the motorist drove into the yard of Eastfield Farm. He got out of the car and approached two men – Ted Wilson and his son, Alan. Not knowing their relationship to the victim, he described to them what had happened. Ted telephoned the emergency services at once, unaware that the victim was his wife.

Tilsley and Blake were waiting by the crime scene when the Wilsons arrived. Ted saw at once that the dead woman was Margaret, his wife. As they stood there, shocked and feeling helpless, a passing nurse stopped her car and got out. She examined Margaret briefly without disturbing the scene; she found no pulse. At approximately that time, PC Steven Kelly from Driffield Police Station was in Burton Fleming, checking the credentials of a young man who had been selling goods door to door in the village. The man's paperwork turned out to be in order, and PC Kelly let him carry on. At that point a call came through from Driffield Police, but Kelly had to go to the edge of the village to improve his radio's reception before he could make out what was being said.

'There's a dead old lady at the side of the road with her throat cut,' he was told.

It seemed highly unlikely, but PC Kelly noted the location and drove there in his van. The sight of Margaret Wilson's body shocked him. The nurse said she had carried out a brief examination and had found the woman to be dead.

'Has anybody any idea who she is?' PC Kelly said.

Alan Wilson nodded absently. 'She's my mum.'

PC Kelly suggested that Alan sit in the police van, then he spoke to Tilsley and Blake about what they had seen. Supervised by the Control Centre at Hessle, PC Kelly next set up a major crime scene. He covered the body with a blanket, put cones around the area where it lay, and moved the witnesses to the opposite side of the road. He then noted where the Montego had stopped, after which he made out a proper crime scene log, listing those who had entered the outer circle, the inner circle, and the area where the body lay.

As the day wore on and the light faded, PC Kelly's efficient one-man enquiry grew into a full-blown murder investigation. A forensic medical examiner and a consultant pathologist both examined the body at the scene and agreed that death had probably been caused by one of two major knife wounds. Detective Inspector John Curry from Beverley Police Station was the first detective to arrive. After assessing the scene and arranging for a tent to be erected over Margaret's body, DI Curry called out three Victim Liaison Officers to look after Ted, Alan and Heather Wilson. A press officer arranged for the Montego's description to be circulated, while a Scenes of Crime Officer examined the immediate murder scene and made a comprehensive photographic record. Polaroid photographs of the victim, plus three plaster casts of shoe impressions from the grass verge, were sent to the Forensic Science Laboratory at Wetherby. Another Scenes of Crime Officer went to the mortuary in Hull and made preparations to photograph the post-mortem examination.

By late afternoon house-to-house enquiries were being conducted in Burton Fleming, Rudston and at a number of outlying houses and farms. Meanwhile, Detective Chief Inspector Martin Midgeley established an incident room at Driffield Police Station. This was designated a Category A enquiry and was manned accordingly – thirty detectives were assigned to work full-time on the case. Since the crime had been committed just ten miles from the North Yorkshire Police Force border, two of their detective constables were brought into the operation and assigned to the enquiry team. HOLMES computers (HOLMES is an acronym of Home Office Large Major Enquiry System) were installed in the incident room to impose order on the inevitably large volume of statements and other evidential material the case would generate. Back at Burton Fleming, a caravan was set up as a mobile incident room, and by the end of the day the crime scene had been completely sealed off. In view of the shock and anxiety the murder was bound to cause in the small community, the authorities decided it would be sensible to establish a conspicuous police presence in the village.

During the early hours of Friday morning, at the Spring Street mortuary in Hull, Dr John Clark, a Home Office pathologist, carried out a post-mortem examination of Margaret Wilson's body. He found that she had been cut twice, across the chin and across the throat, probably with a very sharp knife. The weapon had been drawn across her throat with such force that it had damaged her spine. There was also a bruise on the back of Margaret's thigh where her attacker had apparently used his knee to bring her to the ground. The efficiency of the crime led detectives to believe that the killer could have had experience in the armed forces.

That same night, as news of the murder spread, witnesses came forward and made statements. Edith Morton told police she had turned her car on to the road to Burton Fleming at approximately 3.25 that afternoon. As she drove along, she saw a white car pulled up on the verge. The driver, a man, got out as Edith drove past and began walking in the direction of Burton Fleming. She did not see his face. A little further on, she passed Margaret Wilson, whom she knew, also walking towards the village. In the rear-view mirror she glimpsed the man from the white car walking behind Margaret, who did not seem to be aware that he was there. Edith thought no more of it until she heard about the murder.

Jack Lewis was the driver who had been flagged down by David Tilsley and asked to raise the alarm. He made a statement saying that just before he had been stopped he had seen a light-coloured estate car, the size and shape of a Montego, travelling south in the direction of Rudston.

Alex Bristow owned a service station at Thornholme, a few miles south-east of Burton Fleming. He heard about the murder during the afternoon and remembered Margaret Wilson, who had been one of his mother's friends. Bristow rang the police to say that when he heard the suspect was believed to have been driving a white or light-coloured Montego estate car, he immediately recalled that on the last day of December 1994 – a Saturday, less than six weeks earlier – he had sold a silver Montego estate car for £1,800 to a man from Driffield called Derek Christian. He had paid part in cash, the balance by cheque.

Next morning, at nine o'clock, Detective Superintendent Tony Corrigan headed a briefing meeting in the incident room at Driffield.

A major priority was to create a list of people to TIE (trace, implicate, eliminate). Two detectives were assigned to run a local inventory of white Montegos on the PNC. A psychologist at Wakefield Prison was meanwhile preparing an offender profile as a matter of urgency. A thorough search of the crime scene had already been organized, and it was hoped that this would turn up the murder weapon. As for media coverage, Superintendent Corrigan decided that for the time being it would be best to withhold details of Margaret's injuries from the press, so that only the perpetrator and the police would know that he had cut her twice. Speculation about the killer at that point was broad and relatively unfocused: the police believed the attack was too powerful and vicious to have been committed by a woman, and there was a feeling that whoever had done it may have had possible links to the military.

After the meeting, the Wilson family were visited and assured they would be kept fully informed of developments as the murder enquiry progressed.

'The contact with the family was the point that really emphasized what we were trying to do,' said Detective Inspector John Curry, who had been the first detective at the scene. 'At the end of the day, Margaret Wilson was their mother, wife, grandmother.'

The murder had touched every household in the community, and for some their village would never again be the haven it had seemed until then. 'The public in Burton Fleming couldn't understand why it had happened,' said DI Curry. 'She was tremendously respected in that village, and they were absolutely stunned. This man who had done it was still out there, and the question was: can it happen again? People lived in that area with a real fear for a long, long time.'

The press were briefed, and Heather, Margaret's daughter, made a television appeal that would be transmitted on BBC local news programmes. Early on Friday morning, the Force Plan Drawer had been brought in to plot out the area surrounding the spot where Margaret had been killed. While working on his plan, he came across a knife roughly twelve yards from the spot where Margaret had been found, which put it halfway between the body and the place where the car had been parked. The knife arrived at the incident room around midday. It had a five-inch blade with a black stain; dusting had produced no fingerprints, but Superintendent Corrigan was pretty sure it was the murder weapon. DC Nigel Ling made a sketch of the knife and then began the process of tracing its origin. Knowing who had manufactured the knife and for what it had originally been used would help the team to learn about where the attacker might have acquired it and possibly what he did for a living. The knife itself was sent to the forensic laboratory.

Local publicity and door-to-door enquiries produced more witnesses over the next few days. A number of them reported seeing a white or silver Montego estate, some of the sightings being before the murder, some after. Mary Knight remembered that she drove behind a Montego going at such speed that by the time she got to Rudston it had disappeared. A villager new to the area, Trudy Barton, told the police she had seen a white Montego drive past her house three or four times between 1.30 p.m. and 3.30 p.m. on the day of the murder.

'We had been seriously considering buying one ourselves,' she said. 'I recognized the model straight away. Each time he went past, it was as if he was prowling – that's what really drew my attention.'

She was quite certain that the car had been white, with a black plastic trim. The inside was probably grey, she said. As for the driver, if she recalled correctly he was somewhere over thirty, dark-haired, perhaps with a stubbly chin. She thought he had been wearing a green waxed jacket.

The forensic lab reported that they couldn't identify the black stain on the knife from the murder scene. DC Ling had meanwhile discovered that the knife was made by a company called Adams, who supplied professional-quality knives to nineteen companies in the area. Their biggest local customer was McCain's of Scarborough, manufacturers of pizzas, oven chips and other food products. In the previous nine months, McCain's alone had bought over 1,300 knives identical to the one found at the scene of the murder.

When the psychologist's offender profile arrived, it said that the killer was probably in full-time employment and used a knife at his work. It was likely that he was in a long-term relationship and living within twenty-five miles of the murder scene. He could possibly be an ex-soldier. To bolster his self-esteem, he may have kept a souvenir of the killing.

Following up the statement of Alex Bristow, the service-station owner who remembered selling a Montego to a Derek Christian, two detectives were sent to Christian's house at Driffield. A silver Austin Montego estate car was parked outside the house, and the registration number tallied with the number supplied by Alex Bristow. One of the detectives remarked that although the car was silver, in bright sunlight it looked white.

One of the main purposes of the detectives' visit was to fill out a Personal Details Form (PDF), which would contain, among other details, Christian's physical description, his family background, his employment record and his account of where he was at the time Margaret Wilson was murdered. Throughout the meeting Christian appeared calm and relaxed. The officers described him as slim, with a goatee beard, but no moustache. He told the officers that the clothes he was wearing were the ones he wore on 9 February – a black and blue nylon coat with the logo 'King' on one sleeve; beneath that a purple and green fleecy jacket; underneath that was a green sweat-shirt with a Carlsberg logo on the front; he also wore blue jogging trousers and a black, woolly Sheffield Wednesday hat.

'I wear these clothes to work every day,' he said.

In addition to the work outfit, he had a long, green padded coat, which he kept in the car and sometimes wore when he was driving. The statement of one of the farm workers said it looked to him as if the killer was wearing a green body warmer; Christian's padded coat was green with purple sleeves.

Overall, the detectives thought Christian gave a good account of himself. He was locally born, thirty-one years old, an ex-soldier who had left the army eighteen months earlier. He was married with two children, but the marriage was foundering and he lived part of the time with his parents, the rest of the time at home with his wife and children. He worked at McCain's potato factory in Scarborough; his father-in-law, an engineer there, had got him the job.

Christian's account of his movements on 9 February was that he had worked the 7 a.m. to 3 p.m. shift at McCain's that day, and at 3.05 p.m. he had clocked off. He was in his car and moving off by 3.10 p.m. He drove home on the B1249 from Scarborough to Driffield by way of Foxholes and Langtoft. He was alone all the time and at no point did he stop until he was home. The time of his arrival was 3.45 p.m. – he knew that, he said, because he always looked.

A few of the detectives on the team were interested in Derek Christian because he had no proof that he was elsewhere when Margaret Wilson was murdered, he *did* have the right kind of car and he also worked at McCain's. DI John Curry admitted that Christian was always at the back of some officers' minds, including his own. 'He wasn't the only one,' he said; 'we had a number of people who could have committed the murder, but the clue we didn't have was something that pointed directly to one individual.'

After evaluating Christian's relevance to the enquiry, Superintendent Corrigan and other senior officers decided they had no grounds for an arrest – as DI Curry said, Christian was just one of several men who loosely fitted the bill at the time. His statement was logged into HOLMES.

Two more important witnesses came forward – Anne Young and her mother, Beth Ray. When they heard a radio report of the murder, they recalled being out in Anne's car on Thursday afternoon; near Burton Fleming they had seen a car travelling in the opposite direction at speed. Anne said she got a good look at the driver. She later helped a police artist make a drawing of the man she saw.

At this stage, the main priority of the investigation was to complete the house-to-house enquiries; it was considered important to wait for results from further forensic tests on the knife before committing to poster campaigns and other tactics to stimulate public involvement.

Meanwhile, there were other suspects to be investigated. A car-theft crew from Hull were known to specialize in Montegos; they were investigated vigorously but had no connection with the murder. Another Montego specialist was eliminated from enquiries almost at once, because he already happened to be under police surveillance. The police could account for his movements until 2.30 p.m. on 9 February; it was thought unlikely he would have made it the thirty-eight miles to Burton Fleming in time to commit a murder.

A couple of other known criminals in Hull were put under scrutiny. A stolen car, a Metro, had turned up there the day after the murder, and a knife similar to the murder weapon was found inside. The man who stole the car was soon traced and arrested, but the investigation led nowhere, and both the thief and the owner of the car were eliminated from the investigation. In the second case a man in Hull was arrested after information was received about a white Montego hidden in a garage. Again, the evidence didn't pan out. The man was arrested for stealing the car but was eliminated from the murder enquiry.

A local eccentric was anonymously suggested as a possible suspect. He was known to chat up girls in pubs, and he often told strangers he was Australian, at other times African, and that he had been a member of the SAS. He had a conviction for violent behaviour in the United States, and had served three years in prison there. Witness reports said that when the murder story came up on the TV news in a local pub, he had gone quiet and started behaving oddly. He had no alibi, but he didn't have a driving licence either, and nobody had ever seen him driving a car. The likelihood of his being Margaret Wilson's killer was remote, but he was never entirely eliminated from the list of possibles.

Throughout the enquiry the police also looked for links to other active enquiries, such as the murder of a ninety-year-old woman in her own home, and the Oxfordshire murder of Vicky Thompson, but the other current investigations had no credible similarities to the Margaret Wilson case. There was, too, a list of so-called MO suspects, criminals with operating methods similar to Margaret's killer. These included a double-murderer in Preston. When two detectives from the Wilson enquiry eventually went to interview him at a magistrates' court in 1996, he briefly took them hostage, along with his solicitor.

And there was still the possibility of an army connection to be investigated. The nearest military base to Burton Fleming was at Leconfield, near Beverley. Another base at Driffield was semi-operational and in the process of being run down. Major Frank Lindop of the Royal Military Police at York barracks was called in to help with this stage of enquiries. The army authorities were asked for a list of people currently AWOL; what they sent back was a list of every member of the army who had gone AWOL since the end of the First World War.

On 16 February, a week after the murder, the forensic report on the knife was sent to the incident room. It shed no new light: residual traces of blood belonged to Margaret Wilson, and there were no fingerprints. The stain on the blade remained a mystery and further tests were being made to identify it, with a view to discovering where the weapon had come from. A separate forensic report said that alien fibres had been found on Margaret's clothes, but until there was something to compare them with, they were not significant as evidence.

At this point a new suspect entered the enquiry. His name was Joseph Parry. He lived in Burton Fleming, and he worked at McCain's. He had the use of a Montego estate, and he had no sustainable alibi for his whereabouts at the time of Margaret Wilson's murder. Three months previously Parry was beaten up in the pub in Burton Fleming in retaliation for an alleged sexual assault. Although he did at first look like a strong contender for prime suspect, no positive links between himself and the murder could be established. By the end of March he would be almost entirely eliminated as a viable suspect.

One of the villagers, Mavis Gibson, came and spoke to the police at the mobile incident room on the afternoon of 17 February, some time after the house-to-house officers had visited her. She hadn't come forward before, she said, because she had been frightened. On the afternoon of the murder, Mavis had left her house at 3.15 to take her German shepherd dog for a walk. After several minutes walking she turned and went back the way she had come. About then she heard a car behind her, and as it drew level it slowed down. The driver turned his head and stared at Mavis. It was a frightening stare, she said, full of anger. He then drove on and turned into the road to Rudston. Mavis said the car was a large off-white estate, and she believed she had seen a dog guard in the back. What made this sighting so important was that Mavis insisted she had seen the driver's face and remembered it clearly. Next day she was asked to help a police artist to create an impression of the man, just as Anne Young had. This time another artist was used, and the result was very different. After considering the discrepancy between the images, the police decided to use Mavis' version, since her statement had been more detailed and they believed she had seen the man's face for longer.

On 24 February Superintendent Corrigan and others discussed with the production team of *Crimewatch* the feasibility of screening a reconstruction and appeal. The recce went so well that afterwards the superintendent decided they would rely on the *Crimewatch* programme for public response, rather than mount a separate police reconstruction.

A 'Wanted' poster was launched across the east Yorkshire area in early March; it carried the police artist's impression of the killer as described by Mavis Gibson, and a £5,000 reward (put up by Police Crime Prevention and Farm Watch) for information leading to the conviction of the killer. During this period the radius of the ownership-checks on Austin Montegos was widened, a police helicopter began looking for abandoned cars that could not be seen from the road, the hunt for the source of the knife went on as further companies using the Adams knife were contacted, and everybody who had been in the local pub on the day of the murder was finally eliminated from police enquiries. Interim results from the forensic laboratory showed that the stain on the knife blade was not leather, fish scales or cannabis.

The *Crimewatch* appeal was transmitted on Thursday 16 March. During the programme Nick Ross said: 'We're very reluctant, for very obvious reasons, to show murder weapons on this programme. But the detectives are very anxious that we show you this.' He held up the knife to the camera while a police spokesman explained that testing had so far failed to establish what caused the stain on the blade, although they cautiously believed it had been made by continuous cutting of the same substance. Viewers were asked to call in if they recognized the knife and, importantly, if they knew what job it had been used for.

The appeal generated nearly 1,500 calls. Three names suggested for the killer turned out to be dead ends. Most of the calls were about the possible uses of the knife; fortunately for the officers who would have had to check the hundreds of different suggestions, one of the calls was from Alan Wirth, a professor of metallurgy from Sheffield Hallam University.

Professor Wirth knew about the murder before he saw the *Crimewatch* appeal because he had connections in the area where Margaret Wilson died. Professor Wirth had been out when the programme was screened, but his wife, knowing how he liked factual television, recorded it for him. He watched it later that night, and when the Margaret Wilson appeal came on he felt inclined to phone in. When he realized that the actress playing Margaret reminded him of his mother, he rang in as soon as the appeal ended. He spoke to one of the detectives and said that, although he had no idea what had made the stain on the knife blade, he could find out.

Over the next few days samples of knives were sent to Professor Wirth at Sheffield Hallam University. He explained that by using images of the weapon produced by a scanning electron microscope, he could construct a 'fingerprint' of the elements that combined to make the blade *and* the stain. Furthermore, because the microscope at Sheffield was the biggest of its kind in the country, the entire blade could be scanned in one piece, thereby avoiding the need to cut it into pieces.

'The finding would be qualitative, not quantitative,' Professor Wirth said. 'It would reveal what is there, but not how much of it.' He went on to say that given the appropriate amount of time, he could find out how many times the knife had been sharpened, what it had been used to cut – and even the kind of water it had been washed in. Such fine analysis offered the startling possibility of tracing the knife to a particular workplace. Professor Wirth was asked to do what he could, with the full blessing of the enquiry team.

On 23 March Trudy Barton, who had already told the police she saw a white Montego drive past her house several times on the day of the murder, called the incident room with new information. She explained that she had had a dream, following the transmission of *Crimewatch*, and in the dream she had seen the car again, and this time she noted the registration number. Officers checked the number and found that the car belonged to a man with a history of violence: when he was questioned he produced an alibi for the date and time of Margaret Wilson's murder, and it held up. Concerned to understand how Trudy Barton had come by that number, detectives spoke to her again. She told them that in fact she had not had a dream; she had seen the car on the street and thought the driver resembled the photofit picture shown on the *Crimewatch* appeal.

A number of used knives collected from the trimming line at McCain's in Scarborough were shown to Professor Wirth at Sheffield. They carried remarkably uniform staining on the blades. Making a careful comparison of these knives with the murder weapon, Professor Wirth found that they matched almost exactly. Further tests would be necessary to pinpoint or eliminate McCain's as the source of the murder knife, and in the meantime, on 25 May, vegetable tests on new knives got under way. These tests were aimed at demonstrating the distinct differences between stains left by various organic substances when they came in contact with steel. A variety of vegetables were brought to the laboratory – sprouts, celery, swedes, rhubarb, beetroot. These were sliced with fresh knives that were left embedded in the vegetables for ninety-six hours. At the end of testing, electron micrographs showed that different vegetables left very different patterns of debris and structural alteration on the blades. An odd incidental discovery, made during experiments with other foodstuffs, was that mozzarella cheese will cause steel to disintegrate in fourteen days.

Because it seemed increasingly likely that the murder weapon had come from McCain's, Derek Christian was taken to Driffield Police Station and shown a picture of the knife and asked if he recognized it. He said he had never seen such a knife before. His co-workers at McCain's would later say that he could not have done his job without using one of the knives – and besides, they were lying about all over the place at McCain's, so no one could miss seeing them.

A number of officers on the enquiry were uneasy about Christian, but they didn't feel they could proceed any further against him at that point. There were factors linking him to the murder, but they had more to do with ingrained police instinct than with specific clues. It was also true that some officers thought Christian was less likely to be the killer than certain other men still on the list of MO suspects.

Margaret Wilson's body was released by the coroner and her funeral took place on 21 June. In her will she had instructed that she be cremated, but because the murder enquiry was still in progress she had to be buried, since the opportunity for a second post-mortem had to be kept open. At the funeral the police made a surveillance video of the mourners. Later it was checked to see if anyone unexpected had shown up, but there were no surprises.

By the end of the month Professor Wirth had proved that the murder knife had been used to cut potatoes – the microscopic pattern within the stain was indisputable. He had made comparisons of knives from nineteen companies in east Yorkshire, and only McCain's knives bore that particular stain. To clinch his case, Professor Wirth had also made analyses of water from each site; only the samples from McCain's produced the characteristic changes he had found on the murder weapon.

Derek Christian worked at McCain's, but so did nearly a thousand other people, and all of them would have had access to knives of the kind that killed Margaret Wilson. All McCain's former employees, therefore, and all their current employees, plus all visiting contractors, would have to be checked out.

The mass interviewing of McCain's current staff began on 4 September. It was a huge undertaking and called for Portakabins to be set up in the yard to provide space for officers to conduct their questioning. Inevitably, Derek Christian was among those due to be interviewed, and he made his statement a week after interviewing began. He seemed relaxed and untroubled, and a female detective noticed he winked at her from time to time. Later it would become clear from the information gathered that of all the employees at McCain's, Christian was the only one who owned a Montego and took a southwards journey home, past the murder scene. A number of detectives also noticed that although he now had a moustache and a fuller beard than before, he strongly resembled the photofit picture they were using. Back at the incident room, an officer held up a works ID picture of Christian alongside the photofit, and everyone in the room agreed that Christian could be their man. But there was still nothing substantial that could be used to connect him with the murder.

In mid-November DI John Curry attended a lecture on offender profiling, given at Hull University by DC Simon Wells of the Metropolitan Police. DC Wells was a member of the Bramshill Crime Faculty (Bramshill in Hampshire is a Home Office training establishment), an expert group set up to provide offender profiles and to investigate and establish links between serious crimes. After the talk DI Curry spoke with DC Wells about the Margaret Wilson case, and Wells suggested he put together a team to take an objective look at the enquiry.

A month after that meeting, a group from the Crime Faculty went to Driffield, and one of their number, Detective Sergeant Gary Shaw, addressed the Margaret Wilson enquiry team. He said that his own team had looked at what was available – no distinct suspect and rather too many, no one with previous convictions for that kind of crime. All of the data accumulated to date had been examined and weighed, and the Crime Faculty felt that the enquiry team should concentrate their investigative energies on Derek Christian. The Faculty had identified his probable link to the case on the basis of locality, car and workplace. DS Shaw advised the team to get to know the man inside and out, particularly the quality of his family ties, the number and nature of his friendships, his financial standing, and his attitude to women.

'We'd been going just under eleven months,' said DI John Curry, 'and we had a number of people who could have committed the murder, who were good suspects, but we still didn't know who it was. What the Crime Faculty did was refocus us, in a way. What they enabled us to do was to look more closely at Derek Christian, to look at areas of Derek Christian that may provide an answer.'

Superintendent Corrigan assigned DI John Curry to lead a team of two officers – DC Mike Allibone and DC John Thirkettle – to create an exhaustive profile of Christian. They had to find out everything about his background by sifting his school records, checking job references, investigating work performance, studying army records, questioning friends, probing family situations including particular feuds or loyalties – the team had even to look for any fluctuation in his finances that might suggest the murder of Margaret Wilson had been a contract killing. As emphasized by the Crime Faculty, they were to determine his attitude to women and find out if anything woman-related had been troubling him on 9 February. Because the enquiry was now working on limited resources, and because Superintendent Corrigan was already fighting to prevent staff reductions on the team, the detailed profiling of Derek Christian was allotted three months, no longer.

In late January 1996 the enquiries into Christian's background centred on the Military Records Office at Chichester, and a true turning point in the enquiry occurred when the military discipline papers came to light. They showed that Christian, who had joined the army at sixteen and left at thirty, had twice been court-martialled for violent behaviour towards women. He attacked a woman at a dance hall in Germany, and later, while based in Cyprus, he broke into the female army quarters, where he threatened and attacked the female duty officer. Both attacks had been described as motiveless and violent. In all, Christian was disciplined on three occasions, court-martialled once and served time in the Colchester glasshouse. His status as a suspect in the Wilson case had gone up several notches.

A second *Crimewatch* appeal was broadcast on 24 January to coincide with the anniversary of Margaret's murder. Two hundred response calls were received, but no significant new information was put forward. Nevertheless, the police felt the programme had been of value in keeping the public conscious of the crime and aware that it was still unsolved.

The process of mass questioning at McCain's was still under way, and by now the detectives were talking to sub-contractors. On 21 February Tina Barbour, a young, female HGV driver, was interviewed. Prior to this time the detectives had been told by one of McCain's staff that Tina and Derek Christian had been having an affair. When she was questioned on the point, Tina denied it. She told detectives that she had fallen into conversation with Christian one day at the potato input area. She found him friendly, but said as time passed he appeared to have misconstrued her open manner. She had sent him a birthday card; he had sent her a couple of cards too, and left notes in the cab of her lorry. She wasn't interested in a serious relationship and was careful not to give Christian her address or telephone number. She said that one night in 1995 (this was after the murder) Christian telephoned her a few minutes after she had arrived home; he said he was in a phone box near her home and asked her if he could call round to her house. Alarmed at the thought that he had followed her home, she put him off. Christian later claimed that Tina had invited him to her house, and that she cooked him dinner.

After listening to that testimony, the detectives were concerned for Tina's safety, so for the next session of questioning they arranged to meet her away from McCain's, in a lay-by. By early March they had grown worried enough to put a personal alarm in Tina's house. Shortly afterwards, detectives learned from Christian's estranged wife that she had assumed for some time that Tina Barbour was his girlfriend; the same was also believed at McCain's, where Christian had openly bragged about his 'affair' with Tina.

Christian was kept under close surveillance. In early March the enquiry team felt it was time to start planning his arrest, since the violent profile that had emerged, combined with the evidence of the car, the easy availability of the weapon, and the opportunity, made him the prime suspect. They consulted the Crown Prosecution Service (CPS) who, responding to a concern of Superintendent Corrigan that there might not be enough evidence on which to arrest Christian, confirmed there was.

On Sunday 24 March 1996 police teams called at Derek Christian's house and at the home of his parents. He was in bed at his own house in Driffield, where he had been living off and on since the partial separation from his wife. He had not been interviewed officially by the police since September 1995 and had no idea he had been under surveillance since then. He was therefore badly shocked when DC Mike Allibone cautioned him and told him he was under arrest for the murder of Margaret Wilson.

In the meantime, Christian's parents' home at Bridlington was thoroughly searched by the police. Items of clothing which generally matched descriptions given by witnesses were seized; these included jogging pants, a sweatshirt and a fleecy jacket he had worn on the day he was first questioned. In his bedroom officers found a copy of the *Hull Daily Mail*, open at the appeal published to mark the anniversary of Margaret's murder; it was headed 'Who is Hiding the Killer?' The date on the paper was 7 February, Christian's birthday.

At the police station, Christian was cautioned again and DC Wally Youngman asked him if he wanted a lawyer to be present. He said he did. John Batchelor, the duty solicitor, was called to the police station.

The interview was conducted by DC Wally Youngman and DC Mike Allibone. It was monitored from an adjacent room by DI John Curry and DS Gary Shaw, using the remote speaker, which only ever switches on when the tape machine is recording. During the interview Christian behaved calmly, answering every question without hesitating, giving his answers at length and often including irrelevant details. He was a good talker, never lost his temper, paced himself well, and could obviously think on his feet, which was perhaps a legacy of his army training. He could always remember what he had already said, and showed signs of being ruffled only when questions he had already answered were asked again. Both interviewing officers noticed that he avoided eye contact and would always look a fraction past their heads. Throughout interviewing, he stuck to a consistent line: he had gone to work as usual on Thursday 9 February 1995 and had clocked off at 3.10 p.m. He got into his car in the car park and drove home, using the same route as always, and arrived at 3.50 p.m. In repeating the story several times, he never once hugged himself as people will often do when they are being defensive. Even so, Mike Allibone said he was convinced this was the man who had committed the murder; he knew it as soon as Christian answered the first question, smoothly and in quite obviously rehearsed detail. Both officers felt that, overall, Christian remembered too many insignificant particulars to be convincing. It seemed as if he had spent months thinking over and refining what he was going to say. It was also noteworthy that he never once complained about being held in custody, and he never protested his innocence.

Between interview sessions, Christian was allowed fresh air and exercise in a small yard between the station's custody area and the main police building. He was supervised during these times by a matron, who took him food and lit his cigarette when he wanted to smoke. She told the detectives afterwards that she had looked after many criminals, murderers included, but no one had ever given her the creeps the way Christian did, especially the way he looked at her.

The questioning tended to go in circles, adding nothing to the basis of a prosecution case. Circumstantial evidence pointed at Christian as being the killer, but it lacked the substance to support a charge. An extension to his custody was applied for and was granted, but on the evening of Monday 25 March he was unconditionally released.

'I would say it was probably the lowest point in my fifteen years in the police,' said Mike Allibone. 'It's someone that you're interviewing for the most serious offence there is… To see that person walk out of the police station, and knowing that he's the person who committed the offence – you really wonder whether you've done your job properly.'

Hope of nailing Christian for murder still lingered, however, and the clothing recovered from his parents' home was sent for forensic examination. The two interviewing officers and others on the team had little doubt that Derek Christian had murdered Margaret Wilson. He remained classified as a suspect.

The following day Christian's solicitor called the incident room. He said his client wanted to change part of his statement. An appointment was set for 10 April, the soonest date the original interviewing officers could be available. There was a fluttering hope among the enquiry team that Christian planned to confess. On the due date he appeared at Beverley Police Station with his solicitor, John Batchelor, and was interviewed by Wally Youngman and Mike Allibone under caution and on tape.

Christian now delivered a different version of his movements on the day of the murder. His wife's parents, Mr and Mrs Green, had been moving from Scarborough to a house only a couple of hundred yards away from Christian's marital home in Driffield. According to the revised version of events, Mr Green rang Christian at McCain's to ask him to help move new linoleum, which had been delivered to the Greens at around midday on the day of the murder. Christian said he had left work at 3.10 p.m. and had driven straight to his in-laws' old place in Scarborough. There he loaded a roll of lino on to his roof rack and drove with it to the new address in Driffield. The Greens had followed him in their own car. Christian then left his car at the Greens' new house and walked the 200 yards to his own house. He got into his second car, which was a Rover, and drove to the bank in Driffield, where he used his credit card to draw cash from the machine at 4.06 p.m.

This was a hard alibi to challenge: it was corroborated by Mr and Mrs Green, who genuinely believed the story to be true – and the cashpoint detail tallied. The police also discovered that Christian had written a cheque in the local supermarket at 4.31 p.m., apparently after doing his weekly shopping. Mr Green was certain of the date, 9 February, but Mrs Green said the move could just as likely have taken place on Friday 10. Mrs Green added that on the journey they had seen the aftermath of an accident. The police were able to show that this accident had not happened on the date she said, but a month later, on 10 March, when Christian had been helping them move carpet and had taken the same route as before. But that flaw in the testimony made little difference. The alibi stood, and it was a good one.

Because Christian wasn't under arrest, the detectives were not allowed to question him, but they did ask him why he hadn't come up with this story at the first interview. He replied that he had forgotten all about the lino episode until his father-in-law had reminded him.

Listening to the depressing details later, Detective Chief Inspector Martin Midgeley, who had set up the incident room and was now dogged by dwindling manpower on the enquiry team, took it on himself to check phone bill records with British Telecom. Since Christian alleged that arrangements for moving the lino had been made on the telephone, DCI Midgeley asked BT for itemized bills for the Greens' and Derek Christian's telephones. After being put on hold for a long time, DCI Midgeley was told by a BT representative that unfortunately the Greens' bill for the relevant period had been lost.

A few days later DI Curry had a call from Robin Falconer, a forensic scientist. The DI had left the investigation following the arrest and release of Derek Christian and moved to the Child Protection Unit, but he was still actively involved with the case. Falconer called him directly to say there was crucial new evidence. Falconer, who had been described as articulate and not excitable, was excited enough to say that the evidence was 'very, very significant'.

He reported that he had matched nine alien fibres from Margaret Wilson's coat with Derek Christian's fleece jacket. Three were green polyester from the body of the jacket, three purple polyester from the sleeves, and three purple acrylic from the jacket cuffs. Six fibres were on the front of her coat, three on the back. Testing was still going ahead, so this was an interim finding, but Robin Falconer considered the matches to be conclusive and felt he should pass on the good news straight away. A further eight fibres, he added, could potentially be matched. (The final count from Margaret's clothes would be seventy-eight fibres, every one of them microscopically distinguishable as being from Derek Christian's clothing. This was an outstanding figure, since it is unusual in any enquiry to produce a matched-fibre count that reaches double figures.)

Everyone involved in the case was present when Falconer came to the incident room and officially announced his findings. It was one of the rare high moments in the enquiry and a tremendous boost for morale. Persistent doubts and suspicions about Christian had been vindicated, and at last the team were of one mind. When the briefing was over, they went straight to the Spread Eagle in Driffield to celebrate.

By the middle of September the investigation appeared to have gone as far as it could. Superintendent Corrigan, DCI Midgeley and

DI Curry took the accumulated evidence to the CPS and then to a lawyer, to check that even if nothing else were gained from subsequent interviews or enquiries, they would still have enough to charge Derek Christian with murder. They were assured that they certainly had enough to charge Christian and bring the case to court.

Christian was arrested for the second time on 25 November 1996. He was clearly startled and told the arresting officers that he had thought it was all over long ago. Later he was interviewed at Beverley Police Station, where he was told about the fibre evidence. He said he couldn't explain that. When the questioning was over, he was formally charged with the murder of Margaret Wilson. Next morning he was charged again at Driffield Magistrates' Court and remanded in custody at Hull Prison.

Predictions varied about the strength of the prosecution case. The scientific evidence was immaculate, and Derek Christian's unstable and violent attitude to women could be demonstrated beyond any doubt, but he did have two powerful alibis which strongly suggested he couldn't have been at the scene when Margaret Wilson was murdered: Trudy Barton still maintained that she had seen a white Montego estate drive past her house three or four times between 1.30 p.m. and 3.30 p.m. on the day of the murder; the in-laws, Mr and Mrs Green, were ready to testify that, at the time the murder took place, Christian was helping them move lino from Scarborough to Driffield.

A few weeks before the trial was due to start, DC Wally Youngman was talking on the phone to a BT engineer about a matter unrelated to the case; when he happened to remark that it was a shame BT had lost a bill that could have been crucial to their case, the engineer said flatly that bills couldn't be lost. He took the details and said he would see what he could do. Six days later he called DC Youngman and told him that he had found the missing bill, and was about to fax through a copy. When it arrived, Youngman studied it excitedly. One entry seemed to jump out at him: at 4.10 p.m. on 9 February 1995 a call had been made from the Greens' home in Scarborough, which meant they could not have been in Driffield at that time, as they had maintained. A little further investigation revealed that the call had been made to a furniture store in Scarborough and was probably about details of the Greens' house move. DC Youngman rang DCI Martin Midgeley to tell him the good news.

The detectives met the defence lawyer to request an interview with the Greens. It was granted, and after the facts were explained to them, Mrs Green said she must have been the one who made the call; nobody else ever used their phone and besides, if they hadn't been over at Driffield, then Mr Green would have been at work. Mrs Green was embarrassed and apologetic. The alibi was withdrawn. Derek Christian reinstated his original alibi of going straight home after work on the day of the murder. It was thought likely that the moving of the lino from Scarborough to Driffield took place the day after.

The trial finally opened on 14 November 1997 at Leeds Crown Court. The prosecution brought forward Professor Wirth, who presented his detailed evidence about the stained knife blade clearly and persuasively. Robin Falconer's testimony about the seventy-eight alien fibres was succinct and thoroughly convincing. The only worrying factor for the prosecution was the evidence due to be given by Trudy Barton. If her story was believed, then it meant she had seen another car whose driver could have been the murderer; the prosecution barrister admitted he had worries about the damaging effect her evidence could have on the case.

When the time came for Trudy Barton to testify, she told the court the story she had told all along – that looking across the pond outside her kitchen window, she had seen a white Montego estate, apparently prowling, three or perhaps four times between 1.30 p.m. and 3.30 p.m. on the day of the murder.

The judge said he would like to know the distance between the

Bartons' kitchen window and the roadway on the far side of the pond, and he told the defence he wanted the answer by the following morning. The police thought they should measure the distance too, so DC Youngman planned to take home a tape measure and go out after dinner to the Bartons' place. He forgot the tape measure, however, and drove to Beverley Police Station to pick one up. As he entered, the desk officer told him that Trudy Barton's husband was on the phone. Wally took the receiver and identified himself. Mr Barton said that on the way home from court in the car, Trudy had broken down. She had admitted inventing her whole story, her motive apparently being that she wanted to be of some help to the community she had only recently joined.

Next morning the police met the prosecution barrister to tell him what had happened. Copies of a statement from Trudy Barton, taken by two uninvolved Special Branch officers, were formally presented to the court. When trial proceedings resumed later that morning, the judge announced that the defence needed to re-call a witness. Trudy Barton went into the witness box and admitted that her previous testimony was false. The defence asked for a retrial. The judge turned down the request.

Derek Christian's own appearance in the witness box did him no credit. When questioned about his movements he was dogmatic over times and dates; he didn't appear to allow for the possibility he could be mistaken about such details. When the prosecution barrister asked him if he could always remember times of events or situations that were long past, he said yes, he could. The barrister then asked whether, in any given week, he could remember the times he got home every day in the previous week, and Christian again said yes, he could. That drew suppressed laughter from the court.

On Tuesday 2 December 1997 the jury took two hours to return a verdict of guilty on Derek Christian. He was sentenced to life imprisonment for the murder of Margaret Wilson.

Following the trial, the investigating team were commended by the judge; on 12 May 1998 they received a Chief Constable's commendation for their patient and dedicated work in bringing Derek Christian to justice.

After more than two years of contact with every knowable aspect of Derek Christian's personality, detectives involved in the investigation concluded that he had wanted to know what it was like to murder somebody. His history of violence against women made the gender of his victim a foregone conclusion, and with no specific axe to grind his choice was inevitably random. He left work on 9 February 1995 intent on murder. Mavis Gibson was probably his first target, but he was put off by her big dog. The next woman he saw happened to be Margaret Wilson. By a chilling coincidence, at the time Margaret was attacked her identical twin sister was walking south a couple of miles away on the same road, and Derek Christian must have driven past her.

rebuilding
the truth

At ten o'clock on the morning of 7 June 1996, the discovery of a body in a shallow grave started one of the biggest murder enquiries ever conducted by Hampshire Police. The grave was less than two feet deep and was in a field on Little Abshot Farm near the Hampshire villages of Titchfield and Warsash. The discovery was made when a human arm was dragged up by a tractor driver ploughing the middle of the field. He had dragged the plough right over the body and had detached the arm before he saw anything. A few minutes later the police were called.

By seven that evening a forensic team had carefully recovered the remains from the ground and transferred them to a mortuary. The weather had been hot, and the body was fairly badly decomposed, but it was clearly a man, naked from the waist down. He wore a counterfeit Nick Faldo sweatshirt with the name Pringle on it, although Pringle had not in fact made the shirt. His left ear was pierced. He was 5 feet 4.5 inches tall and weighed about 140 pounds; and was estimated at that point to be aged no more than fifty. They had no idea of his race because his body was so badly decomposed. The body had been buried in a Millets sleeping bag, and also in the grave there was a chunni, a piece of floral-patterned cloth 80 inches long by 44 inches wide. The chunni is an Asian garment similar to a sarong, and is also worn as a headscarf or sash band. In the case of the man in the grave, it was big enough to have been worn as a dhoti – the Hindu loincloth – if indeed it had been his. A Cambridge entomologist examined bluebottle larvae and other insect matter found on and around the body and estimated the likely time of death at around 24 May. A number of serious dents at the back of the dead man's skull, administered with a blunt instrument, were later established to have been the cause of death.

A fifty-strong murder squad was assembled for the investigation, which was code-named Operation Plato. The squad was headed by Detective Chief Inspector (now Detective Superintendent) Mike Lane, who admitted at the outset that they had a difficult job ahead of them, not only in solving the murder but in identifying the victim. The tractor and plough that uncovered the body had done a lot of damage, and the dead man's face was unrecognizable. The brief description of the body, furthermore, did not match any missing-person records from the area. Plans were already under way to call in the services of Richard Neave, Artist in Medicine and Life Sciences at the University of Manchester. Neave is renowned for his talent in reconstructing human faces on copies of unearthed skulls.

Following the necessary preliminary forensic work, the dead man's skull was taken to Manchester and handed over to Neave, whose first step was to make a plaster mould. He then took careful measurements to make sure that both skull and replica were exactly the same size. When he was satisfied that they were proportionally identical, he set to work. In explaining his craft, Neave pointed out that the skull is in effect an armature, providing the complete basis on which the face and head are built. In portraiture of the head, to ensure that the picture truly looks like the face of the model, the proportions have to be absolutely correct: the space between the eyes, the distance between the eyes and the mouth, the size of the nose and its placement in relation to the other facial elements. With a skull, there is no more perfect armature to work on, because it already provides the exact proportions of the vanished face.

As work on the project progressed, basic anatomical science would be used to develop the tissue and muscle groups over the surface of the copied skull. A clay face would eventually grow outwards. Published tables of soft-tissue measurements would help to ensure that the amount and thickness of tissue built onto the skull at any given position would be consistent with known standards and norms. It is not guesswork. Neave maintains that the combination of measurements, statistics and basic anatomy allows the face to develop of its own accord.

The difficult part is rebuilding the unknowable areas. The skull will provide the proportions and dimensions; what it can't do is tell what the tip of the nose looked like, or the expression of the eyes, or the shape and density of a person's eyebrows, or whether that person had pronounced forehead creases. A bonus with this skull was that the ears had been preserved, and prior to cleaning the skull had been topped by a shock of intensely black hair. Neave would incorporate this information into his sculpture.

Back in Hampshire, Mike Lane was trying to figure out why Little Abshot Farm had been chosen as the place to bury the murdered man. It is remote and not easily reached from either Southampton or Portsmouth. Lane's feeling was that the killer was someone who knew the farm, although that scarcely narrowed the range of possible suspects. The owner of the farm grew extensive crops of vegetables, which he supplied to supermarkets, and he was a large-scale employer of subcontracted workers from a number of minority ethnic groups. During the year prior to the discovery of the body there had been about 400 people working at the farm, most of them foreign nationals and a large proportion of them transient. All of them, as well as the inhabitants of Titchfield and Warsash, plus many hundreds of holiday-makers in the district, had to be interviewed as part of the police effort to find out who the dead man was, and who had killed him.

In Manchester, Richard Neave had already inserted glass eyes and tapped numerous tiny metal pegs into the plaster copy of the skull; the pegs acted as indicators of tissue depth as he began building the clay structure of the face on to the skull. The main pitfall of the work, he said, was in having any preconceptions of what the individual looked like. The thing to do was to let the skull and the science dictate his movements. When he began building the nose, which he described as a contentious area, he remarked on how broad it was, and that the face overall was obviously not standard Caucasian. As he worked steadily, building up the layers of clay, a human likeness began to emerge. There were a number of distinctive features, possibly useful in making an identification. The man had a large overbite, which meant that when he smiled or opened his mouth his two top front teeth would have overlapped his lower lip. There was also a skull deformity which made the face slightly lopsided, this possibly arising from a childhood accident or illness which caused one side of his face to grow faster than the other.

Once Richard Neave had finished with the original skull, it was taken to Dr David Whittaker, a forensic dentist at the University of Wales College of Medicine in Cardiff, who would try to provide the police with more information about the identity of the dead man. The teeth, Whittaker pointed out, contain a lot more inherent information than any other part of the body. The reason for this is that teeth grow over many years; information is built into them over the sequential period of development, and it is never lost. Where there is a problem of identity, it is Whittaker's view that the teeth, which retain their information for many years after the death of the body, provide the single most useful avenue of investigation.

Whittaker began with an examination of a slice of a tooth extracted from the skull. Under the microscope, a sliver of tooth reveals many tiny tubes running from the pulp at the centre of the tooth through the dentine, which is a bony substance under the enamel that forms the main constituent of a tooth. With time, these tiny tubes fur up, much as water pipes do, and the number of such furred-up tubes is a reliable indicator of a person's age. When Whittaker had taken a count from the specimen, he transferred the figure to a printed scale made up previously from many teeth of known age. This method of estimation told him that the dead man's age had been somewhere between thirty-nine and forty-four years.

That was only a beginning. Looking at the teeth in general, Dr Whittaker noted that they were very markedly worn, which is usually an indication of contaminants in the diet, such as grit and sand. That sign, plus the lack of decay in the teeth and the overall shape of the skull, inclined Whittaker to the view that this had probably been someone from the Middle East, or perhaps Eastern Europe. There was also evidence on the skull that an upper incisor tooth had been lost before the man died. That would be an important identifying feature if dental records were ever found.

A lower left molar had been fitted with a gold alloy crown. On analysis this was found to be 21 per cent gold, 35 per cent silver, 22 per cent palladium, 16 per cent indium, 4 per cent copper and 2 per cent zinc. Only one manufacturer in Britain produces this type of alloy, selling it to 179 dental technicians around the country who then, in many cases, sell it on to dentists. This was another potential avenue of investigation.

A month after the discovery of the body, the murdered man's identity was still not known to the police. Mike Lane decided to go public with Neave's facial reconstruction, distributing posters showing two colorations of the head, one of them a general Asian skin tone, the other more in keeping with an Eastern European complexion.

Another month passed without the dead man being identified. Dental technicians were being interviewed, and then Mike Lane approached *Crimewatch* and talked to them about publicizing the case. On 3 September an appeal was broadcast, featuring a plaster copy of the reconstructed head and both colourized images. The appeal produced seventy telephone calls, one of them very specific and the only one to suggest a name for the dead man. With a name to go on, the police soon tracked down a dentist in East London with a registered patient of the same name. This was the first glimmer of a breakthrough, although he was already on the list of dentists the police were interviewing and they were only ten days away from visiting him. The relevant dental records were found and taken to Dr Whittaker in Cardiff for comparison with the radiographs he had already made. They were a match, and, interestingly, there was a written record of damage and temporary repair to a lower left molar, and the eventual fitting of a three-quarter gold alloy crown; this all tied in with the forensic examination. Dr Whittaker was now happy to confirm the dead man's identity. He had been a 39-year-old Sikh, Harjit Singh Luther, who had lived in Ilford. He had never been reported missing.

Mike Lane decided to bring in for questioning people who had been close to the victim. They lived in Southampton and Ilford and included the man's girlfriend and her husband. The idea was that search warrants would be issued and, when the people living at those addresses were brought to the police station for questioning, the police would search the premises cautiously, looking for a crime scene, specifically a scene of violence – blood, disorder, whatever. If a crime scene was found, the officers discovering it were cautioned to go no further, but to report the finding and then withdraw. A specialist team would then go in and perform a full forensic search.

The four people who were arrested were questioned and released. In the meantime, Mike Lane went to the dead man's home in Grange

Road, Ilford, which had already been sealed by forensic experts. He said he had reason to believe that Harjit Singh Luther had been murdered at that address. After spending a short time inside the house talking with forensic investigators and being shown around, Lane emerged and said he was pretty sure now that this was the place where the victim had met his death. What his team had to do now, he went on, was to fill in the background on Harjit Singh Luther and learn all they could about the kind of man he was, the style of life he led, and find among the details a clue to the motives that drove someone to kill him.

As soon as the dead man had been identified, a large part of the enquiry team moved their headquarters to Ilford Police Station. Among their searches, the police found a photograph of Harjit, which confirmed the accuracy of Richard Neave's reconstruction. Officers interviewed his neighbours, his drinking friends, anybody in fact who had known Harjit, probing as deeply as they could into his background. He had been living in Britain for several years, and by all accounts he was an ordinary, likable man. He had a girlfriend, also Asian, with whom he had a child. He had worked for a double-glazing firm where his relationship with his workmates had been harmonious. However, as time passed the Ilford investigation began to reveal that Harjit had led a very complex life. Born in Aden, he lived in India for a time and got married there, then came to England on his own in 1991. He formed a relationship with a woman somewhere around 1992, and in 1995 she had a child. In August 1995 Harjit went back to India, allegedly to arrange a divorce from his wife there. When he came back he found that he was locked out of the house in Ilford and his girlfriend was gone. A short time later he discovered that while he was in India his girlfriend had been married. It was a quickly arranged marriage to another Indian, and the couple had moved to Southampton. There followed a sequence of events during which the woman came and went between the two men, which required her to travel a good deal between Ilford and Southampton. In the meantime, the woman's husband was involved with another woman. The situation was not so much a love triangle, Mike Lane remarked, as a quadrangle.

In late November, after following up a number of leads, the police found the red Cavalier car in which they believed Harjit's body was transferred from Ilford to Hampshire. Traces of his blood were found in the boot. At his home, a fingerprint was found belonging to Baljit Singh Rai, the husband of Harjit's girlfriend, Manjit Kaur Rai. This couple now became the prime suspects in the case. Investigations revealed that Manjit had been telling anybody who asked that Harjit had gone back to live in India. Manjit had also made two trips to India and visited Harjit's relatives to tell them that he was in India. To support the story, everything belonging to Harjit had been removed from his house. A great deal of evidence was accumulating to indicate that if Manjit was not implicated in murder, she was certainly involved in a conspiracy. Her husband, police discovered, was an illegal immigrant desperate to remain in England. Although he was seen in Ilford by several people at about the time Harjit may have disappeared, there was still no certainty about the date of the murder.

In order to try to establish the date, the police began analysing over 4,500 telephone calls made from Harjit Singh Luther's home in Ilford and from addresses in Southampton. On Harjit's telephone there was evidence of plenty of activity until 10 April, followed by a period of four days with no telephone activity at all. Then, on 15 April, there was massive activity on Harjit's phone: eleven calls were put through to India in one day, nine of them to the same number. The only time afterwards that the same telephone was used was on the day Harjit's body was discovered in June. On that day there was more frantic activity on the lines, to both India and America. Mike Lane saw it as significant that at the time the calls were made there had been no release of the story to the press. That could have meant that someone who knew about the murder had spotted the police activity at Little Abshot Farm and was warning others.

Eight months after the body was found, in February 1997, Mike Lane travelled to India, to the Punjab. He wanted to prove that Manjit Kaur Rai was lying when she told people that her boyfriend, Harjit, had gone back to live in India in late April of 1996. By that time, it was pretty certain he was already dead.

While in India, Lane also wanted to check on some telephone calls. At a local telephone exchange he set about identifying the addresses of the numbers called from the murder scene. One address was the home of the mother of Baljit Singh Rai, the male suspect. Lane wanted to prove that this was the number called nine times on 15 April the previous year. To do this, Lane called his office and arranged for them to call the mother's phone – in other words, he wanted to know if one of the numbers the enquiry was interested in actually connected to the woman's address. And it did.

A rather touching meeting took place between Lane and Harjit's wife and her mother in their home village. Harjit and his wife had been married for sixteen years, the mother-in-law explained. Harjit had worked as a driver, but in 1991 he decided to go to England and try to make his fortune. That was the last time they had ever seen him. Later, Lane travelled to the place where Harjit's relatives lived and took statements from several of them. These interviews with the relatives were video-taped in case they were needed as evidence in an English law court. The relatives confirmed that Harjit had not been seen in the region since 1995, when he had briefly visited India – although on that occasion he had not seen his wife. Any plans he might have had for obtaining a divorce were obviously not followed through.

Two weeks after he returned to England, Lane was ready to put his suspects under arrest; they were, of course, Baljit Singh Rai and his wife, Manjit Kaur Rai. Following the arrests, the couple were questioned separately, in Punjabi, with their solicitors present. Mike Lane and his team listened to a translation in a room adjacent to the interview area. Throughout questioning, both suspects denied any involvement in Harjit's murder. The questioning went on for three days, then finally the couple were jointly charged with the murder of Harjit Singh Luther.

It was fifteen months later, on 3 June 1998, that the trial opened at Winchester Crown Court. On the first day, Manjit Kaur Rai astonished the court by admitting openly and without pressure from the prosecution counsel that she had watched Harjit Singh Luther being murdered, and that she had later watched his body being buried at the remote Little Abshot Farm in Hampshire. She said she had been too frightened to tell the police. Over succeeding weeks the whole story was put before the court. Manjit described her life with Harjit and their little daughter. Everything had gone well with them, she said, until Harjit failed to get a divorce. While Harjit was still in India, Manjit's family talked her into a hurried marriage with Baljit Singh Rai, an illegal immigrant, who married Manjit for no other reason than to avoid deportation to India. She told the court that she knew how shocked Harjit was when he came back from India to discover she had left him and married another man. Manjit's marriage was unhappy, a sham, and her husband refused to stop seeing his long-standing girlfriend. Periodically, Manjit went back to her boyfriend in Ilford, and because of the way this appeared to be jeopardizing their marriage – and therefore, as Baljit saw it, his future in England – he decided he would eliminate his rival from the picture. On the night of 10 April 1996, Baljit arrived at Harjit's house in Grange Road, Ilford, and let himself in quietly using a spare key. He climbed the stairs to the bedroom where Harjit and Manjit were asleep in bed, and there he battered Harjit to death with a hockey stick. The wall was spattered with blood, identifying that room as the site of the murder; Baljit later made a further blunder by telephoning his mother over and over again from the scene of the crime. Baljit and Manjit drove together to Hampshire with the body of Harjit in the boot of the car, and together they buried him at the farm where Baljit had once worked as a labourer.

Baljit Singh Rai was found guilty of murder and was sentenced to life imprisonment, with the additional ruling by the judge that he be deported on completion of his sentence: 'This country has no need of criminals of other nationalities.'

The jury of seven men and five women found Manjit Kaur Rai not guilty of murder. They took the view that she was an Asian woman, therefore virtually the property of her husband, and that she had acted under exceptional duress.

The judge, Mr Justice Cresswell, described the police investigation as 'truly remarkable'.

The story had a curious twist. Five months after the murder, Manjit had a baby boy. Expert evidence produced during the trial disclosed that the father was not her husband, as Baljit himself had believed, but the murdered boyfriend, Harjit Singh Luther.

death of an innocent

The charity called Victim Support provides support and assistance to over a million people every year. Victims and witnesses can call on a network of local schemes where they will find trained staff and volunteers ready with emotional support, information and practical help in any of the many crises brought about by crime. Wilbourne Williams, fifty-six, known to friends and acquaintances as Herbie, was a trained volunteer working with Victim Support in Southwark, South-East London. One day in July 1998, Herbie himself became a tragic victim of crime.

'He was a very quiet, dignified, calm sort of person,' said Gerry Forde, co-ordinator of Victim Support at Southwark. 'I'm sure he was just the type of person somebody who was all upset would love to meet. He was genuinely just a nice person, one of life's good guys. And he was really interested in helping others.'

Around noon on Wednesday 15 July, Herbie boarded a number 185 bus on Vauxhall Bridge Road. He sat next to a man who, according to other passengers, appeared to have been drinking. When the man threw a bottle out of the bus window, Herbie gently remonstrated with him, telling him he shouldn't do things like that. The man responded by telling Herbie to mind his own business. A witness said he then threatened to cut Herbie.

Herbie tried to calm the man, but he had become angry and looked as if he might start swinging his fists.

'Just leave me alone,' Herbie said. 'Please leave me alone.'

'I'll cut you...'

The man fumbled in his pocket, saying he had a knife. Herbie got up and walked to the front of the bus. The man followed him. The bus pulled in at a stop on Vauxhall Bridge and Herbie got off. The man continued to follow him and when Herbie turned and tried to fend him off he drew a knife.

'I'll stab you!'

The man then slapped Herbie on the face, and when Herbie raised a hand to fend him off again the man stabbed him in the chest. Herbie fell to the ground, and his assailant ran off. Several people followed him. He ran down the Albert Embankment through Spring Gardens and disappeared in the vicinity of Kennington Lane. In the meantime, Herbie was treated for blood loss and was flown by air ambulance to the Royal London Hospital. On arrival there he was pronounced dead.

A police circular described Herbie's killer as a black male aged between thirty-four and forty-five years old, of medium height with a stocky build. He had medium-length unwashed black hair flecked with grey and a full, matted beard. He was scruffily dressed in a 'puffa' jacket, a mustard-coloured shirt and dark trousers.

'I never in my life saw something like that,' said a shocked witness. 'Just stabbing somebody, in broad daylight... an unprovoked act. At that point I said no, he's not going to get away with this.'

But the attacker eluded some very determined attempts to follow him, and the police were left with little to go on.

'I just couldn't contemplate Herbie, of all people, being involved in any sort of an argument,' said Gerry Forde. 'Afterwards it became clear that he did all the right things – he got up, moved away from the confrontation, left the scene.' Forde's shock was echoed time and again by witnesses who could scarcely believe that something so senselessly barbarous had happened on a busy London street, and all because of an upset over an empty bottle. Just as unbelievable was the killer's disappearance. Of forty people on the bus at the time of the incident, fifteen came forward with descriptions of the attacker, but none of their testimony enabled the police to make an arrest, or even gave them a list of suspects.

At a briefing of officers, DCI Mike Petra put the situation plainly. They were looking for a dangerous and perhaps unbalanced individual strong enough to have killed Herbie Williams outright with a single thrust of a knife-blade into his chest. The murder weapon had not been recovered, and there was no usable forensic evidence. The killing had been captured on CCTV, but it was very difficult to make out the attacker. As he ran off, he dropped a folded pair of trousers, which may have been stolen, but that was not a clue that appeared to lead anywhere. DCI Petra made no bones about it: there was very little to go on, and if there was to be even a hope of gaining any more, they would have to do a tremendous amount of work.

The first priority was to have the suspect's description circulated as widely as possible. Officers were told to focus on the killer's matted beard, unwashed hair and generally scruffy appearance. While the description was being circulated, a search would have to be started – the most determined of the pursuers had followed the killer into the Vauxhall Estate.

'If we're to stand a chance of finding this man,' DCI Petra said, 'we'll have to begin by knocking on every door in that area.'

It was a daunting prospect. There were 500 flats, plus shops, garages and offices. Petra told his officers to divide up the work and to go very carefully. They were looking for a man who had killed somebody for practically no reason at all, and there were no grounds for thinking he wouldn't do it again.

The case was to be plagued with wrong turnings and red herrings. One man who claimed to have seen the attack was questioned closely, and at some length, only to be revealed as a publicity-seeking time-waster who had learned all he knew about the case from a police poster on a bus window. Another man, whose appearance closely matched the suspect's, was picked up by an alert uniform officer; he was investigated for a considerable length of time until someone noticed that he had turned up on CCTV in another part of London at the time Herbie Williams was killed. There was also a telephone call from a resident of Stornoway who believed the killer was living there; this suspect turned out to be a white Irishman.

A problem that occasionally complicates police procedure is the embarrassment of riches that can arise from widespread appeals for information. The investigating team on the Herbie Williams case not only circulated the description of the man they wanted, but they also gave presentations and briefings at many police stations. In the end, their vigorous campaign resulted in their having too many responses to cope with. Every one had to be followed up, and the results were often startling. One man cited as the killer turned out to weigh about twenty stone, and he had a long white beard. A trip to Derby to examine some allegedly relevant CCTV footage showed an unidentified man in a linen suit and panama hat who resembled, as someone remarked at the time, Hannibal Lecter in the final scene of *The Silence of the Lambs*.

In the second week of the investigation a resident on the Vauxhall Estate, Martin Gibbs, was taken to Tooting Police Station for questioning. He was a known shoplifter with previous convictions for stabbing and handling firearms. Until the day he was brought in, he had also fitted the description the police had been circulating, but now he was bald and beardless. He had obviously done a thorough job of altering his appearance, which only intensified the detectives' suspicions about him. When they searched his flat, however, they found no clothes even similar to those described by witnesses, and there was no trace of a weapon. Gibbs had to be released, and in the meantime there were a further 150 men waiting to be eliminated from enquiries.

As the system became clogged with suspects, it grew more and more important to know exactly what the killer looked like. The main witness, Mr English, was not pleased with the photofit prepared by the police; no matter how they altered it, the face continued to look too young. DS Gary Flood suggested having the photofit aged and so the witness was finally taken along to the National Missing Persons Helpline to meet Di Cullington, an expert in ageing human features – a skill necessary when trying to locate people using outdated photographs. By patiently responding to the witness' description of how the photofit image varied from the face he had seen, Di finally produced a version of the face which the witness believed was a ninety-five per cent accurate likeness.

While that was a step forward, it seemed to put the police no nearer to finding the man they were after. They tried getting the media involved and made a particular effort to have an appeal broadcast on *Crimewatch*; this was set up for September. Nick Ross introduced the slot as 'a reconstruction of the sort of scene everybody dreads'. Its impact was immediate, and the response, as DCI Mike Petra said, was magnificent. Well over 300 calls were received. Nick said afterwards, on air, that the reconstruction must have been the one to cause viewers most anguish that night. At long last, it seemed, good-quality intelligence was coming in. Six people seeing the revised photofit picture called in and identified the man as Martin Gibbs, the suspect who had altered his appearance prior to being arrested.

One piece of information turned out to be crucial. A man who had been offering stolen goods for sale to drivers at a local minicab office had also been overheard confessing to stabbing a man in the chest after arguing with him on a bus. A detective went along to speak to the drivers, who identified the man as Martin Gibbs.

Gibbs was detained and put in a line-up for an identification parade. The main witness, Mr English, was invited to pick out the man he had seen kill Herbie Williams – if he believed the man was in the line-up. Mr English looked long and hard, and finally said the man he had seen was not there.

But even though Gibbs was not picked out, DCI Petra decided it was time to put him under surveillance. 'All along, my big worry was that this man could potentially strike again.' The issue of public safety was paramount. A watch was kept on Gibbs night and day. Then one night, as he walked past a plain-clothes surveillance officer, he pulled out a long-bladed knife. The officer told him to take it easy. Gibbs waved the knife at him. 'I thought you were going to jump me,' he said. 'I've got this knife… any funny business I stab you.'

Gibbs walked on, but that incident, clearly recorded on tape, was enough for DCI Petra. 'I would have liked more time,' he said, 'but once he'd pulled a knife on a surveillance officer then the decision was made and he was arrested. I felt then that with the statements we had after the *Crimewatch* appeal, and with the work the officers had been doing behind the scenes, we now had enough, certainly, to charge him.'

That, of course, was only a beginning. The police had their man safely in custody, but a mountain of work lay ahead. 'The fact that you've charged somebody is a long way before you get enough evidence to ensure a conviction at the Old Bailey. I knew we couldn't afford to take the foot off the pedal – that's when the real work started.'

The accumulated evidence had to be sifted and ranked in order of relevance. The evidence against Gibbs was hardened while 200 other suspects were systematically eliminated from enquiries. As the weeks passed the police case grew as a mounting pile of boxes and files. Statements were double-checked, data and dates were confirmed time and again; every detail was treated as unreliable until it had been verified at least twice.

'As we got near to the trial,' said DCI Petra, 'I thought our chances were good, but not fantastic.'

Then five days before the trial was due to start, a call went through to the incident room at Tooting Police Station to tell the investigating officers that Martin Gibbs had changed his defence. He was now admitting that he killed Herbie Williams, but that it was an accident.

'With what we had,' said DCI Petra, 'there was no way he could claim it was an accident.'

In court, witnesses testified to hearing Gibbs brag about committing a murder. Surprisingly powerful evidence came in the form of the low-quality CCTV footage of the killing. Despite the lack of clarity, it was obvious that one man, the shorter, did nothing but defend himself, while the other kept on the attack until the shorter man fell. It was a moving and telling re-creation of Herbie's final moments.

Gibbs's behaviour in court did nothing to help his case. Throughout the prosecution's opening he kept shouting: 'Lies! Confounded lies!' When he was asked at one point if he had meant to kill Mr Williams he said: 'Everyone has to die some time.' On another occasion, when he was asked a serious question, he retorted: 'What do you want? Blood? Poke it up your nose hole.' At other times he writhed on the floor.

The matter of Gibbs's fitness to plead was controversial. A psychiatrist who saw him four months before Herbie Williams died had said he should be sectioned – that is, compulsorily detained in a psychiatric hospital in accordance with the provisions of the relevant section of the Mental Health Act. But his social worker decided not to have him sectioned. Those who privately argued that his sanity was impaired had to face the counter-argument, that Gibbs was sane enough to ditch the knife used in the killing as well as the clothes he wore that day.

Martin Gibbs was eventually sentenced to life imprisonment, with the recommendation that he spend a minimum of nine years behind bars. Of his victim, Herbie Williams, Gerry Forde said: 'It's a shame that he's gone, because he could have done an awful lot more good for victims of crime. Certainly, a number of people he did help are the better for having met him.'

Ian Phelps, the handcuff robber who covered the distinctive tattoo on his ear with make-up.

The holdall found in Phelps' bedsit that contained the handgun and handcuffs he used to commit robberies.

DJ rapist Richard Baker who was given four life sentences for a string of rapes and sexual attacks.

Leslie Salter who viciously attacked his elderly victims.

The scene at Enid Poole's flat after Salter had beaten her unconscious and ransacked the place.

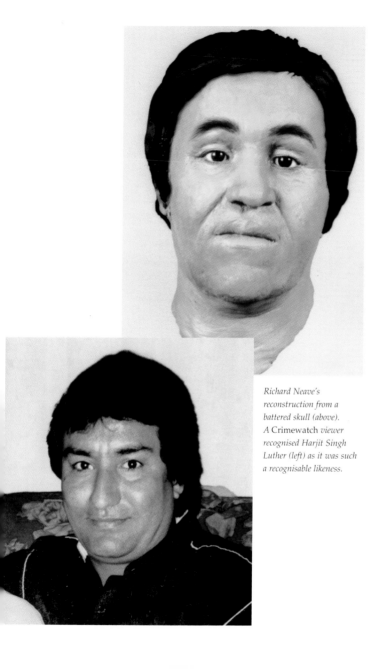

Richard Neave's reconstruction from a battered skull (above). A Crimewatch viewer recognised Harjit Singh Luther (left) as it was such a recognisable likeness.

The artist's impression of Martin Gibbs (above) and Martin Gibbs (right). Six Crimewatch *viewers correctly identified him as the man who killed Herbie. After the murder he tried unsuccessfully to alter his appearance.*

Jean Barnes was a multi-linguist and one of the first women to graduate from Cambridge University.

A forensic test on Jean Barnes' lino revealed a match with David Munley's shoe.

The cheque forged by David Munley to pay the milk bill after he killed Jean Barnes.

Dear Milkman,

I am sorry but I am going into Hospital on Monday 26 July. Then I will be going into a Nursing Home.

Therefore could you please leave me the Bill until Friday 23rd and a loaf today.

Thank you for your kindness.

J H Barnes

9, Tennyson Road
Worthing.

The letter to the milkman which helped focus the enquiry and point the police in Munley's direction.

The squalid attic where Merlyn Nuttall was sexually assaulted, half-strangled, stabbed and left to burn.

Merlyn's description of the distinctive tracksuit Ferrira wore at the time of the attack.

An artist's impression of Merlyn's attacker that helped to identify Tony Ferrira.

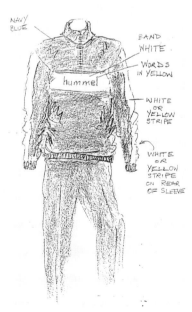

Steven Reid (left) who killed
Elizabeth Stacey (below) told the
police he didn't want to die alone.

greed

The town of Worthing in West Sussex, fifty-eight miles south-east of London, is a seaside resort, immortalized by Oscar Wilde in *The Importance of Being Earnest*. With its mild and sunny climate and its position overlooking the English Channel, Worthing has for many years been a popular residential town for retired people and those who used to be known as 'persons of good position and family'. Jean Barnes lived alone there for more than forty years. On the evening of 26 July 1999, Mrs Woolvern, a partially sighted lady whom Jean used to read to over the phone and who lived opposite Jean, called the police to say she was concerned because Jean wasn't answering the telephone. The two women were friends, and they had devised a coded method of telephoning so that each would know it was the other calling. Mrs Woolvern, just returned from a few days away, told the police that something was surely wrong, otherwise Jean would have answered the phone straight away.

Two WPCs were sent round to Tennyson Road to try to raise Miss Barnes. At the house there was no response to their knocking. They went along the side of the building and broke a windowpane so they could raise the sash. One of the officers climbed inside and made a quick reconnaissance of the downstairs area. The place was full of broken-down-looking domestic appliances, mismatched furniture, ornaments, bundled clothes and stack upon stack of newspapers. An unpleasant odour hung in the air. When the officer opened a bedroom door the smell grew stronger. On the floor, covered by a blanket, was the decomposing body of a woman, her feet jutting out at the edge. The adjacent wall was spattered with blood. Carefully raising the corner of the blanket, the WPC could see that the woman's head had been beaten in.

The officers alerted CID, and before long the house and garden were cordoned off. Scenes of Crimes Officers worked inside and out as Detective Superintendent Steve Scott, the officer in charge of the investigation, gathered what information he could.

'It was very difficult to find out about Jean Barnes,' he said. 'She was a reclusive lady – over the last twenty years she hadn't gone out very much at all. In fact, the photograph we used for the reward posters was twenty years old. She had a nephew who lived out of the area, and I think she had a godson who lived up in Iceland. There were friends in the area that she saw irregularly... perhaps they would call by and do some shopping for her. But really it was Mrs Woolvern and maybe another neighbour, and that was about it.'

Interesting facts about Miss Barnes did come to light, however. She had been one of the earliest female graduates of Cambridge University, emerging as a gifted linguist who was fluent in six foreign languages. Her plans to marry had been crushed when her fiancé died in the Second World War. After that she immersed herself in her career in the Civil Service, working as a translator and interpreter for the Foreign Office and other government bodies. Over the years of her retirement, and up until the time she died at the age of eighty-seven, she did make occasional contact with her nephew and a handful of friends locally. For recreation she read, dabbled a little in rose-growing with the help of an Italian gardener, and listened to the radio and to classical music she had collected on tapes. She did *The Times* crossword every day and never threw away a copy – her bundled archive of newspapers, stored piecemeal throughout the house, dated from 1926.

A post-mortem examination, performed late on the day that her body was found, revealed that Jean Barnes had died from multiple skull fractures resulting from nine or ten blows to the head, inflicted with a blunt instrument. The blood splashes on the wall in the room where she was found were directionally upward, indicating that the blows were delivered to her head while she lay on the floor.

'The pathologist thought that perhaps the body had been there for three, four, five days,' said Detective Superintendent Scott, 'but later on an entomologist who did some work thought that perhaps it could have been as long as twenty-one days.'

It was hard for the pathologist to estimate the time of death with any confidence, because it was very warm and humid outside but cool in Jean's house and the rate of decomposition was impossible to reckon. The entomologist had been brought in because the body had been infested by the larvae of scuttle flies (also known as hump-backed flies), and their stage of development could be useful in estimating how much time had elapsed since the body had become receptive to their presence – which would probably have happened only a short time after death.

'That made it quite difficult for us to make our enquiries,' said Scott, 'because people can remember what they were doing for one hour in a certain day, but what they were doing over a two- to three-week period is of course difficult to remember.'

There were other confusing pointers to consider when estimating the time of Jean Barnes's death: she made her final telephone call on 10 July; her *Radio Times* was found turned to the page for 12 July, and a neighbour believed she saw Miss Barnes in the garden on 15 July.

'As we started to develop the investigation looking for a motive, looking for when she had been out and who she knew,' said Detective

Superintendent Scott, 'we discovered that she had reported a burglary in January, when she'd had a barometer and two paintings stolen. The officers who attended couldn't find any forced entry. Naturally, the Crime Prevention Officer went round, and she changed her locks and took other security precautions.'

That was not the only time Jean Barnes had called the police to complain about something suspicious happening. In February she reported that as she was putting out her milk bottles at about 3.45 one morning, she was attacked and had her spectacles broken. 'Then, on 23 April, she had a very strange phone call from a man. He pretended to be from her bank, and he asked very personal details about her: her date of birth and that sort of thing.' Miss Barnes later told the police after having spoken to the staff at her bank and being assured the call hadn't come from them.

'Then in May she had a credit card and a bank card arrive from the Alliance and Leicester and from Barclaycard,' Scott said. 'She hadn't ordered those, and when we called for the copies of the application forms we saw that somebody else had written those two application forms.' Following that incident, Miss Barnes had her locks changed a second time.

At the beginning of the murder investigation a check of the station log showed that between February and July Jean Barnes had called the police several times to report items – mainly pictures and ornaments – missing from her hallway and stairs. It might have seemed to police officers dealing with her in that period that she was not entirely in possession of her faculties, but Detective Superintendent Scott soon discovered that was not the case.

'When we got called in to the murder investigation, what was quite clear was that while her health may have been failing her mind wasn't. In the early 1990s she had moved around quite substantial sums of money from one account to another to get the best interest rate... She knew what she was about. Even up to two or three months before her death she was speaking fluent Italian to her gardener.'

There had been no evidence of forced entry at the house on Tennyson Road, so there was the possibility that the killer had been someone Miss Barnes knew; either that or she had been prevailed upon to let a stranger walk into her home. Burglary was an obvious motive, because there were many valuable items among the three-storey sprawl and clutter of Miss Barnes's effects. It took four Scenes of Crimes Officers two months, working full-time, to search every room and littered passageway, looking for evidence and making a detailed inventory. From the start, it was obvious to everyone working on the case that there had been recent movements and disturbances among the long-standing clusters of hoarded possessions.

'What we found was that there were obviously things that were missing from the house,' said Detective Superintendent Scott. 'For example, where the dust had been allowed to gather there were templates in the dust where no doubt a teapot had stood, or a clock.'

It did not need a detective to spot some of the signs of purloining throughout the house – light patches on walls where pictures had been, dented patterns on rugs and carpets where chairs and side tables had been removed, and half-emptied shelves in otherwise crammed cupboards and cabinets. A couple of rooms had been ransacked without any effort being made to tidy up the mess afterwards. What puzzled Scott and his team was that other rooms in the house, even though they contained items of considerable value, looked as if no outsider had gone near them. Paradoxes of that kind are the last things busy detectives need. Scott said: 'Because she was reclusive we had no motive at all. As the investigation went on we discovered that she was probably worth about half a million pounds. Now if somebody had known that and known the type of antiques that she had in her house, that obviously became a potential motive for someone breaking in.'

An early lead in the investigation involved a man who had been seen near Miss Barnes' house, telling passers-by that his car was out of action and he needed to borrow £15 to get back home. The police approached *Crimewatch* and asked if they would issue a description of the man, which had been given by several witnesses. The *Crimewatch* team obliged. Almost at once the man went to the police and admitted that he had used that broken-down-car ploy many times, but he didn't know – and didn't want to know – about any murder. After exhaustive questioning, the man's story was believed. He was eliminated as a murder suspect and charged, instead, with multiple counts of deception.

The week before Jean Barnes' body was found there had been a well-attended fair in Worthing. Because police were unable to say exactly when the old woman had died, the enquiry team were obliged to widen their investigation of people's movements to take in traders and known visitors to the fair. 'Of course, that brought in an awful lot of people and an awful lot of sightings,' said Detective Superintendent Scott. 'That meant that we had to check these sightings out. Who were they, who was seen walking their dog, who was seen carrying a carrier bag down the road? It was very frustrating.'

More than 200 officers were involved in the investigation at this point. Local people were being questioned extensively and asked to search their memories for any oddities or even slightly unusual incidents, or visitors, seen along Tennyson Road during July. A breakthrough occurred when Miss Barnes' milkman approached the police with a note that she had left him about a week before the murder was discovered. The note was written on the torn-off back of an envelope, and said that Miss Barnes would soon be going to hospital and thereafter into a nursing home. She wanted to stop milk deliveries, and would the milkman please leave his final bill? The milkman had done as he was asked and later found a cheque for the amount left on the doorstep at number 9.

The police made immediate enquiries at hospitals, nursing homes and among neighbours of Miss Barnes. Nobody had heard of any impending hospitalization or of a move to a nursing home. The note was a fiction and, together with another one that the milkman recovered from a wastebin, was probably a forgery. This development had to be added to the discovery that a number of Miss Barnes' keys could not be found, and that daily papers which were probably delivered after she died had been taken indoors and put on a pile of others on the stairs. It now looked likely that whoever had forged the notes to the milkman had also entered and left the house several times since the murder was committed. This suspicion was reinforced when the police learned that five days before Miss Barnes' body was discovered, a representative of British Gas called at the house; there was no reply to his knocking, but he distinctly heard the sound of a radio or television coming from inside.

For purposes of comparison, a number of samples of Jean Barnes' handwriting were sent to handwriting experts at the Forensic Science Service (FSS), together with the two notes, the cheque left for the milkman, and another recently recovered cheque used to pay Miss Barnes' overdue electricity account.

'What had happened was the letter to the milkman had been written on an envelope that had been sent by Seaboard, the local electricity company,' Scott said. 'It had been ripped open, and the letter had been left on the doorstep. Well, on the first floor in the kitchen was the other half of the envelope, and it married up exactly. Within that was a red reminder for her electricity bill. That also had been paid... We recovered that cheque.'

In the meantime other evidence was turning up at Miss Barnes' house. 'As a result of deploying the forensic officers for such a long period,' Scott said, 'one of the things that we got out of that search for evidence was a foot mark on the second floor on lino. A clear foot mark. That was recovered and sent up for a scientist to look at. On the ground floor there was a tissue in the room adjacent to where her body had been found. That had faint specks of what could have been blood. So that again was sent off.'

Late in August the results of the handwriting checks came back from the FSS. The notes to the milkman and the cheque with which he was paid were forgeries, and the handwriting matched that on the suspect bank applications. The experts did not commit themselves on the sex of the forger, but they did say it was probably a person in his or her fifties, and it looked as if they had made no serious effort to change the characteristics of their own handwriting. While there was still no indication of who had committed the murder, the evidence of the notes and cheques made the motivation pretty clear. Detective Superintendent Scott was convinced that most if not all of the forgeries had been made after Jean Barnes was dead.

'They were written to make people think that she was still alive,' he said, 'and to allow the offender to continue to return to the house and to continue to steal property, even though her body lay in the ground-floor bedroom.'

With that much reasonably certain and the case by now six weeks old, the police decided they could use specialist help to accelerate the process of identifying the murderer. 'We called in an offender profiler,' Scott said: 'Julian Boon from Leicester University. We didn't want to know what the offender had for breakfast or what sort of clothes he wore. What we wanted to know was what type of person would commit this crime.'

The local paper's response to the profiler's arrival was the head-line WORTHING MURDER: CRACKER CALLED IN. Scott said he didn't mind what the newspapers said, '...as long as they say it on the front page, and as long as we get exposure of our murder.'

In introducing himself to the investigative team, Dr Boon said that where he thought he might be useful was in approaching the case from a forensic psychology perspective, which may be different from investigative experience – not better, he stressed, but different.

Different approaches, if well informed, could often produce the same conclusions though for different reasons, and agreement under such circumstances gave weight to the conclusions. If the conclusions differed, then discussion would be stimulated, and discussion generated new ideas, especially when more than one professional perspective was involved.

Boon was taken to the crime scene and shown around. He was given full access to the accumulated investigative data and was present when officers on the team expressed their various doubts and uncertainties about the case. It was not long before Boon began to form an understanding of the kind of individual who might have murdered Jean Barnes.

'What Julian told us was that the person would probably live in the area, that it wouldn't be unusual to see him walking in the street, and that he would have targeted elderly people in the past. Now we put that together with what the handwriting expert told us – that the offender would probably be in their fifties. So we started to build up a picture of who we were looking for: a man in his fifties who probably lived in the area. It wouldn't be unusual to see him walking in Tennyson Road, and he would have targeted elderly people in the past.'

Again Scott applied for a *Crimewatch* slot. This time he was keen to make it a three-strand appeal. First he wanted to publicize the reward – it was £30,000. Then there was the handwriting on the milkman's notes, on the bank applications and on the cheques; Scott wanted the writing to be shown on screen and the various idiosyncrasies to be emphasized. The third strand was MO, modus operandi. It was important that viewers be given an idea of the age, personality and tactics of the person the police wanted to interview: did anyone recognize a fifty-year-old man, living locally, who had targeted elderly people before?

On the night of 16 November *Crimewatch* screened the new appeal. Detective Superintendent Scott was interviewed and gave prominence to the reward, half of it put up by the police, the other half by the estate of Jean Barnes. Then large blow-ups of the hand-writing forgeries were shown, with Nick Ross describing the peculi-arities of style. Finally, the MO: a fiftyish individual who makes his moves on the elderly, bogus phone calls, unexpected bank accounts... did any of that ring bells?

After the programme Scott felt pleased with what had been done. His three strands had been correctly addressed, and they were put across with energy. There had been a reassuring public response, 250 calls, probably because Jean Barnes had been portrayed as a vulnerable human being whose solitary life was callously sacrificed to someone's greed.

'The next morning after *Crimewatch*,' said Scott, 'I was sitting in the hotel looking through the 250 responses. And through this priori-tization process there was one particular call that fitted all the criteria. It was a call from a lady called Mrs Ridpath who lived in Worthing. She could remember using a handyman, David Munley, four years previously, and not only had he worked for her but he'd done jobs for an elderly neighbour, Winifred Smith, who was in her eighties.'

It was in around March 1996 when David Munley started work on the house of Winifred Smith. The job dragged on for six months, with Munley working a day and taking two weeks off, then working another day and having another two weeks off. Over the six months Mrs Smith paid Munley various sums of cash for materials. She wasn't sure how much she had paid; she didn't keep a record. During the same period Mrs Smith noticed that £60 had gone from her desk, and she had no idea what had happened to it – again she put it down to her poor record-keeping. Audrey Ridpath, on the other hand, was a stickler for making accurate records, and she actu-ally did book-keeping for Winifred Smith. It was not long before Mrs Ridpath discovered that someone had taken cheques from various parts of Mrs Smith's chequebook and cashed them, divesting her bank account of a total of £4,000. When Mrs Smith went to the bank to ask how this could have happened, the manager showed her a letter which they assumed had come from Mrs Smith, telling them that she was going into a nursing home and that her nephew, someone calling himself David Armstrong, was authorized to manage her affairs. The matter was never reported to the police.

The first thing to alert Mrs Ridpath was a news item on that evening's *Crimewatch*, as she explained. 'I was watching the early-evening news, and this letter came up. I was astonished to see something that I thought I'd seen before, or something very similar.'

Mrs Ridpath was sure that the handwriting she saw on television was very much like that of David Munley, who three years earlier had invoiced her for £80 for the work he had done at her house. After she had watched the full *Crimewatch* programme she decided to make a call to the studio. Because of the priority status Scott had decided to give her call, members of the Jean Barnes murder enquiry went to her house and interviewed her the next day. They took away Munley's invoice, which she had kept carefully filed.

'Well, this was the breakthrough, really,' said Scott, 'because not only did we have somebody that had targeted an elderly person in Worthing before with cheques and bogus handwriting, but the key words on that letter – "going into a nursing home". We looked again at the letter that was left for the milkman – "going into a nursing home", and then we sent off the handwriting from the Audrey Ridpath invoice and the Winifred Smith account. We quickly realized that the call that Mrs Ridpath had made to *Crimewatch* was the call that we had to follow up.' When enough background evidence was in place, Munley would be arrested. It was discovered, meanwhile, that Munley fitted another slot as a suspect: he was fifty-six years old.

When he was asked later what he believed had prompted Mrs Ridpath to call the programme, Scott said: 'I think she recognized two strands of the appeal. First of all the writing was quite unique.

Nick Ross had made a big play about certain features of the writing. But also, of course, there was the targeting of an elderly person, her elderly next-door neighbour. So two of the strands that we hoped to get out were there for her, and she recognized them and phoned in.'

Another local case which turned up in the meantime involved a man called Geoff Collins of Byron Road, in Worthing, who had died in 1998. Close to the time of his death, someone had made a successful application for a cash machine card in Collins' name, and the card had been used. During the ensuing investigation, which had come to nothing, it was discovered that someone had been filling Collins' dustbin with rubbish, possibly with a view to creating the illusion that he was alive for some time after he had actually died. Consulting the electoral register for the time in 1998 when Geoff Collins died, the police discovered that one of the occupants of a flat in the house where he lived had been David Munley.

There was little delay in the handwriting expert's response this time. He found numerous similarities between the recently submitted documents and those previously sent in connection with the Jean Barnes investigation; those similarities could not have occurred accidentally – therefore, the strong likelihood was that the same person had written them all.

There was an air of excitement and anticipation among the enquiry team. Before the transmission of the *Crimewatch* appeal on 16 November, the enquiry had a suspect roll of 30,000 people convicted of robbery and assault against the elderly. That was a worst-case scenario, but it was not unrealistic, given the lack of solid leads at that time. The first time anyone had brought up the name of David Munley had been when Mrs Ridpath made her call to the studio. First time or not, his elevation to the front of the queue of probables had been swift, mainly because of the use of the same wording on two forged letters and other similarities between the Barnes and Smith cases. Soon after the team spotlight fell on Munley, a Police

National Computer, or PNC, trawl showed that he had one conviction against him – it was for fraud, in 1983.

The trawling continued. Munley's fingerprints were retrieved from the files, and they turned out to match prints found on the letter of 'authorization' sent to Mrs Smith's bank. They were also on the cheque to the Seaboard electricity company. It was discovered that Munley's latest abode was close to Miss Barnes' house.

'He lived 240 yards away,' said Scott. 'And it would not have been unusual to have seen him in the street. He had a small dog that he walked up to the park, and he would have had to walk up Tennyson Road to get to the park. We knew that Miss Barnes had had a dog two or three years previously, which had died. So it's not beyond the realms of possibility that she had perhaps started a conversation with him as he walked up past her house.'

The arrest of David Munley was a co-ordinated operation calling for one team of police officers to pick up Munley and the woman he was living with – assumed to be his mother – and keep them separated for subsequent interview at separate police stations. A second team had to isolate the flat so that its condition and contents remained intact until it could be searched by Scenes of Crimes Officers and detectives. In spite of the numbers of officers involved and the unpredictable reaction of the 'targets', the arrest went smoothly. Munley, a man of small stature and generally unkempt appearance, was taken to Crawley. The woman, who turned out to be his ex-wife, eighteen years his senior, was taken to the station at Worthing.

After more than an hour of careful sifting, the search team at the flat had found no documents with Munley's handwriting on them. There had already been speculation that he might have seen the *Crimewatch* appeal and had decided to edit his belongings. A key found in the garden was checked with the locks at number 9 Tennyson Road, but it didn't fit. Two more keys hidden in the bathroom were also tried at the house, but they wouldn't fit either.

Back at Worthing, Judith Munley was offering no resistance to questioning. She explained to the officers that she had formed an uneasy reconciliation with her ex-husband and had even allowed him to take charge of her financial affairs. Since then she had lost her chequebook, and the bank had told her she was overdrawn. All in all, the woman appeared to be more of a victim of Munley than his accomplice.

On first arriving at Crawley, David Munley complained to the police doctor that he had a headache and that he badly needed to sleep. He was told he could take three hours' sleep before interviewing began, and he was given a couple of tablets of co-proxamol for his headache. The interviewing officers were not pleased about this, but there was nothing they could do.

Julian Boon, the profiler, had warned Detective Superintendent Scott that the offender in this case would be, in his view, a psychopath. He emphasized that he used that term in its correct sense: a psychopath is someone with a personality disorder characterized by extreme callousness, a person with little or no conscience who is liable to behave antisocially to get his own way.

'We'd been told by the profiler that he would probably be a liar,' said Scott. 'And he was. I mean, he would roll out lies about where he'd been or what he'd been doing. He would try to engage the officers in light-hearted banter, but they continued to put their questions to him about movements, about sightings, and about what he'd been up to... But then the officers started putting it to him that antique dealers had just told the police that it was him who was selling them antiques, and that he had made up a story that an aunt either in Suffolk or Norfolk had died, and he was clearing the house out with his brother. He started to realize that we knew more about him and more about his activities than he thought we did.'

As he was confronted with more and more of the accumulated evidence of his wrongdoing, Munley widened the gap between himself and his interrogators. He became stiffer and less responsive, no longer the bewildered innocent but rather the expressionless recalcitrant, denying everything. He denied he had ever been in Miss Barnes' house, he denied he had ever even met her. How his finger-prints and handwriting came to be on incriminating documents he had no idea, and he simply shrugged at the mention of a footprint from Miss Barnes' house, which would eventually prove to be his.

'And he started to clam up,' Scott said. 'He started very much to act like the Prime Minister does at question time and refer us to a previous answer...'

During a break in questioning, approximately eleven hours into the interrogation, Scott was in the kitchen at Crawley Police Station making himself a cup of tea. He was glumly bemoaning the atmos-phere of deadlock that was beginning to surround the interrogation. 'And while I was making the cup of tea my deputy, DI Underhill, came in, and he said: "We've got some news." And as he was telling me he couldn't help smiling.'

During the course of the day the search at Munley's place had spread into the communal areas of the dwelling, which was a permis-sible move, because the search warrant covered the whole house. At the foot of the stairs was a very large meter cupboard, and the search team found a suitcase in there. It contained David Munley's birth certificate and his diaries, so they were now in possession of copious examples of Munley's handwriting. There was also clothing in the case and a tent spike, which could have been the murder weapon, though it turned out not to be. The team then took the suitcase out of the cupboard and found a loose floorboard where it had been lying. They lifted the board and underneath they found Jean Barnes' Civil Service membership card. There was also a broken candlestick that was believed to have come from her house.

Scott could not have been more pleased. They now had property linking Munley with Jean Barnes, and they had Munley's handwriting, so any attempts he might now make to disguise his hand would be pointless.

Not long afterwards DI Underhill brought more good news. Details of Munley's telephone billings had finally come through. The bogus 'bank' call to Jean Barnes in April 1999, asking her for personal details, had come from Munley's telephone.

As the questioning continued, Munley's denial strategy began to fail him. He was being confronted with increasingly strong evidence, so much so that it would have done him less harm to remain silent than to go on making blanket denials. He continued to deny that he had fraudulently obtained a cashpoint card in the name of Geoff Collins, but that was about to be rebutted by photographic evidence: an indistinct picture of Munley using the card would soon be studied by an expert in facial mapping, who would say that the man in the picture was definitely Munley. In other areas of interrogation he lied in answer to questions where the truth would have made him appear less devious – for instance, when talking about the work he did for Mrs Ridpath he insisted he was always paid in cash, unaware that the police had already retrieved the cheque for £80 that she had given him. At the close of the final session of the day, Munley was no longer the flippant, rather patronizing individual who had walked into the interview suite that morning. The questioning had visibly worn him down, and although he was far from being overwhelmed by the experience, he was certainly a worried man.

Before winding up the day's activities, Scott spoke to the officer in charge of Crawley Police Station to alert him that he was going to apply for an extension of the 24-hour period after which detainees usually have to be charged or released. Scott wanted to do this because he needed Munley to have time overnight to understand the gravity of his situation, and then face another, tougher session of questioning in the morning. If the extension was granted, Munley would be questioned about Mrs Barnes' Civil Service membership card, and about the telephone call allegedly from her bank which in fact emanated from Munley's telephone. The search team also needed more undisturbed time to screen the flat and the rest of the house with metal detectors, and to search for buried objects in the garden.

The extension was granted, and in the morning another session of questioning began. Munley appeared even less responsive to questioning than before, stonily denying anything that sounded incriminating, not answering some questions at all. Later that day, 4 December 1999, he was charged with the murder of Jean Barnes. Crawley Magistrates' Court remanded him in custody pending trial.

Before the trial date, two more items of evidence came up positive: the flecks of blood on the tissue from the room next to the one where Jean Barnes died were a DNA match for Munley's blood, and the foot mark, a shoe print found on lino on the second floor, matched one of Munley's shoes.

Finally, at the end of an investigation that had cost £600,000, David Munley went for trial at Lewes Crown Court on 14 November 2000. He pleaded not guilty to murder, eight counts of burglary and six of forgery. The offender profiler, Dr Julian Boon had predicted a guilty plea from Munley, and so had Detective Superintendent Scott. The not-guilty plea was a disappointment, but on the other hand the 200-plus officers working on the Jean Barnes murder enquiry had taken almost 1,000 statements, and now a lot of that material would be properly aired in court, rather than simply being filed away for good.

There were statements from antique dealers who told the court how plausible the defendant had been, talking to them about a house packed with valuable stuff, all of it his aunt's, which would eventually be for sale once he had sorted out the estate. The house, he had elaborated, was in Norfolk or Suffolk, next to a church and had been occupied by his aunt and uncle, who had both been missionaries. When they died, the house had been left to the church and the house contents to Munley and his brother. Munley resisted offers by dealers to view and value the stuff *in situ* – his brother wanted only a few of the pieces, but he hadn't yet made up his mind which ones.

The prosecution were able to demonstrate, without actually saying so, that although Munley was clearly an individual who could pass himself off as normal and affable, he preferred to paint his life and its events the way he wanted them, rather than the way they were. An antique dealer who had previously dealt with Munley said he came into the shop one day in April or May 1999 and in conversation mentioned that he had a bracket clock in pieces in a box at his flat – would the dealer like to go there and value it? He agreed to do that and a time was set. About an hour before the dealer was about to leave, the telephone rang. It was Munley. He told the dealer not to bother coming round; he'd had a representative from Christie's call at the flat, and he had valued the clock at over £100,000. Munley said he was going to sell the clock at auction. About a week later the dealer saw Munley again, and he said he had sold the clock privately for £130,000. The dealer didn't see Munley in the shop for some weeks after that. When he did eventually come in again, he said he had been in Thailand. The dealer didn't believe that, because he had seen Munley around the town.

It was impossible even to estimate how many pictures, pieces of furniture and *objets d'art* Munley stole from Jean Barnes, but many of them turned up in court as evidence, thanks in large part to the diligence of reputable and concerned antique dealers. Munley unwittingly advertised his thefts by leaving labels on the backs of pictures and furniture, some of the labels discreetly publicizing the Manchester Pantechnicon Removal Company in Manchester patronized by Jean Barnes's family in the early years of the twentieth century; other labels bore the name Ricketts, the maiden name of Miss Barnes' mother. Furniture and pictures identified by these labels were sold to five dealers in Worthing during September 1998, clear proof that Munley had been systematically stealing from Miss Barnes for some time – ten months at least before she died.

The forged note to the milkman was read out to a hushed courtroom: 'Dear Milkman, I am sorry but I'm going into hospital on Monday the 26th July. Then I will be going into a nursing home. Therefore could you please leave me the bill after Friday 23rd and a loaf today. Thank you for your kindness.'

'The wicked falsity of the note,' said a journalist who was in court, 'was a hell of a rebuke to Munley. He got some very hard-eyed looks when that was read out.'

The defence did what they could, which was mainly to split hairs. Practically every piece of forensic evidence was criticized as being inconclusive, and even the evidence of the blood on the tissue was challenged – it was heavily suggested that somehow a blood sample taken from Munley after he was charged had found its way on to another tissue which was switched for the original.

Munley was the only witness called by the defence. For seven years until 1991, he told the court, he had worked for a company that specialized in making buildings fire-resistant. When bankruptcy hit the company, Munley bought the fireproofing division and operated it as a one-man business. The enterprise failed, and Munley had to sell his house to clear his debts. Since then he had been a handyman and gardener, supplementing his modest income by dealing in antiques. He said he had never been in Jean Barnes' house. Traces of his DNA found at 9 Tennyson Road had been planted by the police, he said, and that assertion set the tone for most of his testimony. He denied having driven a car since 1997, but when it was shown in court that he had hired a car in 1999, he said that was true, and added: 'It depends what you mean by "drive".' As for the shoe pattern found at Jean Barnes' house which matched the worn sole of one of Munley's shoes, he said that since Marks & Spencer had sold 20,000 pairs of those shoes, another pair could have worn the same way as his.

As the trial drew to a close, the main worry for the police was that the jury might place undue significance on the fact that no murder weapon had been found. In fact, nothing at all had been found to link Munley physically with the murder of Jean Barnes. However, Munley unexpectedly admitted that he had stolen and forged cheques from Mrs Smith, and forged a letter from her to the bank. That surprised the court.

On the seventeenth day of the trial the judge, Mr Justice Alliott, told the jury to go out and consider their verdict. Six hours later they came back. The verdict was guilty.

David Munley was sentenced to life imprisonment for murder, five years for each burglary to run concurrently, and four years for each forgery to run concurrently. The judge made a point of commending Mrs Ridpath for making her call to *Crimewatch*. It was undoubtedly her information that turned the case around and led the police directly to the guilty party.

'There's no doubt in my mind that going on *Crimewatch* got us that vital call,' said Detective Superintendent Steve Scott. He likened investigations to jigsaw puzzles. Clues built up the picture piece by piece. 'I think that Audrey Ridpath's call gave us plenty of the jigsaw.'

merlyn's story

On the morning of 18 February 1992, a day worse than any she could have imagined, Merlyn Nuttall felt no uneasiness or foreboding. What she felt mainly was irritation, for she was running late and twice she had gone back to her flat in Tulse Hill, South London, to collect things she'd forgotten. Merlyn had missed her bus and was now hurrying along Effra Road to Brixton tube station with the breeze sharp on her face.

'Excuse me!' A man approached from a terrace of seedy-looking houses on Merlyn's right. He was black with a neat flat top haircut and wearing a stylish blue tracksuit. He looked seriously agitated. 'Please help me…'

Merlyn paused, annoyed at the new hitch.

'My girlfriend's pregnant,' the man said. 'She's fallen. Can you stay with her while I get an ambulance?'

There was no reason to disbelieve him. He was clearly on edge and there was no hint of threat – even at that early hour Effra Road was busy. Merlyn glanced at her watch. When she looked up, the man was at her side. Ever practical and decisive, she was about to suggest that she call an ambulance while he waited with his girl-friend, but suddenly he took her arm in a tight grip. He turned towards her, letting her see a knife in his free hand. Merlyn froze.

Softly, the man said she must do as he told her, emphasizing the urgency with a jab of the knife-point against her coat. 'Hurry,' he said, and pushed her towards the end of the terrace. 'She's alone…'

He tightened his grip on her arm as he pushed her towards the house at the end of the row. Merlyn tried to stay calm and do nothing to provoke him or make him worse.

The three-storey house at the end of the terrace, number 9, was set back from the others. Overflowing rubbish bins and up-ended boxes of trash and old bottles cluttered the forecourt. The man shoved Merlyn up the nine steps and through the door, which was already open. Windows on either side were hung with torn filthy curtains. In the gloomy passageway the air stank of urine and vomit. Rubbish was scattered about the bare floor, mouldering paper hung peeling from the walls. As Merlyn stumbled towards the staircase, the smell grew more acrid.

'Hang on, honey!' the man called up the stairs, still pushing Merlyn, hurrying her, making her climb. 'I've brought someone!'

They went up five flights, their feet banging noisily on the boards. The man kept yelling as they went, saying it was OK, help was coming. On the top landing he grabbed Merlyn and held her tightly to himself as he kicked open the attic door.

'In there,' he snapped.

She looked into the dim, squalid room and saw it was empty. No girlfriend. Merlyn screamed suddenly. She pushed at the man, tried to shove past and get away from him. He grabbed her by the neck with both hands and squeezed. Merlyn struggled. The constriction on her throat tightened as he tugged at her scarf. She began to choke.

Then, as swiftly as he had grabbed her, the man let go. Merlyn drew in air and staggered a couple of steps, coughing. He put his face close to the back of her head.

'No one can hear you up here,' he whispered.

Merlyn took stock, staying in touch with reality the best way she could. She was in a very small attic with greasy-looking walls, lit by a single lamp in the corner. The sloped ceiling had two blacked-out skylights. On the floor directly opposite the door was a mattress with stained covers; the only other furniture was a low, flimsy table and an old office chair. Bottles were scattered about the floor and on the table, some of them filled with urine. Hypodermic syringes were strewn among the rags and debris littering the bare floorboards. On top of a stinking pile of rubbish an incongruous Harrods carrier bag lay crumpled.

Behind her the man spoke again, telling her to do as he said. She had to look at the wall. Always. 'Don't move unless I tell you.' She was forbidden to look at his face. The brief glance she'd taken when he accosted her was all she had seen of him.

He told her to take off her overcoat. Her hands shook as she started to undo the buttons, then abruptly, before she had the coat halfway open, the man pushed her face down on the grimy mattress. In a frenzy he tried to tear open the jacket Merlyn wore under her coat. He kept yanking at the straining material until finally he tugged off both garments and threw them on the floor. He pulled up her T-shirt, raking his nails across her back. Then he stopped what he was doing and told Merlyn, casually, that he liked the trousers she was wearing.

After a pause he began treating her roughly again, pulling off her clothes, and when the fastening of her bra resisted he literally tore it off her. But moments later calmness descended again: he took off her shoes carefully, and he asked her what make they were. She told him they were Shelly shoes. Her voice shook; she was frightened, cold, vulnerable.

'You got a boyfriend?' he asked.

She lied and told him she had.

'How old are you?'

'Twenty-seven.'

He asked her date of birth. She told him – 17 October 1964.

The inane, pointless talk continued, and after a while Merlyn found she could see the man at the edge of her vision – at any rate she saw his legs, which were now bare. He stood at the foot of the bed. Merlyn moved her gaze, fixing it on her Filofax, which had fallen on the mattress when he first pushed her down.

'What's your job?'

'I'm a fashion buyer,' she said. Remaining perfectly still, she asked a question of her own: 'Have you done this kind of thing before?'

He was silent for a moment. 'No. You're the first.'

She asked why he had picked on her.

'Because I couldn't get a pretty girl like you the ordinary way.'

He moved away from the bed. Seconds later there was the clink of glass on glass and a smell of whisky.

'Move up the bed,' he said.

Merlyn slid further along the mattress. In a low voice he ordered her to touch herself so he could watch. Merlyn simply could not do as he requested and she froze on the spot.

The man flew into a rage. He ordered her to turn over and keep looking at the wall. He threw himself on top of her, and it was obvious he intended to bugger her. She pulled herself away from him, howling, grasping at the bed to drag herself clear.

'Please!' she begged him. 'Please, not that!'

And again his violence dropped away. He stopped, said 'OK,' and moved back from her. 'But listen, if I'm not getting that, you have to let me have something else I want.'

As before, he was explicit, saying she must perform oral sex on him, and in a specific way. Merlyn stayed as passive as she could, enduring the onslaught.

When it was done he got off the mattress and told her to turn over and look at the wall again. She did as he said. 'Can I go to work now?' she asked him. 'I'm late for my meeting.'

Instead of replying, he told Merlyn to pass him a plastic bag lying on the floor near the mattress.

'And don't look round,' he warned her.

But after she had passed him the bag and lay down again she did look round, obliquely, adjusting the angle of her head enough to see him on the perimeter of her vision. He was wearing his tracksuit again and was taking something from the bag. It was a coiled wire with bamboo handles on the ends. It looked like a cheese wire.

Seconds passed. Suddenly, the man's weight come down on the mattress beside Merlyn. He was kneeling over her. As he leaned closer he slipped something under her head and around her neck. It was the cheese wire. He pulled on the handles, making the steel filament bite into her skin and cut off her breathing.

Strength surfaced from somewhere in Merlyn. She forced her fingers under the wire and pulled it a fraction away from her neck. He tugged on the handles again. She screamed as the wire cut into the soft tissue of her right hand, nearly severing her thumb. Even then she kept on, fighting in spite of the pain. With flailing legs and one wildly punching fist she put up enough resistance to propel them both off the mattress and on to the floor.

The wire slackened suddenly as the man knelt and pulled it away from her neck. Skin went with it. As Merlyn lay panting, he straddled her again and began using his fists, pounding her with a torrent of blows that struck every part of her. Merlyn tried to fight back, but the cascading punches were too ferocious to resist.

When he stopped hitting her there was a moment of stillness in the room, then he came at her with a broken bottle. He threw his arm over her shoulder from behind and thrust the spiky glass against her throat. She couldn't break free, but her wriggling and clutching at his arm kept him from landing a blow directly on her windpipe. He jabbed and poked, tearing her neck, stabbing her larynx.

As they struggled on the dirty floor, Merlyn was steadily losing blood, and when the man began repeatedly stabbing the jagged glass on the back of her neck, puncturing the flesh at the base of her skull, her head whirling with the excruciating pain, she passed out.

She came round some time later and felt searing pain in her right hand. She could hear a crackle, and another, the unmistakable sound of flames. Then there was smoke and the closeness of heat. Her attacker had scattered her clothes at her head and feet and Merlyn thought he had set fire to her. In reality, he had set fire to rubbish and clothes next to her. The flames licked close, and Merlyn jerked back her leg. As soon as she moved he was on her again, his arms flailing, beating her. Merlyn felt herself kicked several times, hard, and then he was stabbing the back of her neck again with the broken bottle. She realized that if there was to be any chance of living through this, she would have to play dead. When she was a child, a swimming instructor had commended her ability to hold her breath; she used the talent now, lying motionless and unbreathing.

After a while he stopped hitting her. Sounds came to Merlyn: he was moving around her. Then it was quiet except for the crackling of the flames. She finally opened her eyes a fraction and saw she was alone.

She sat up. The room was filling with black smoke, most of it coming from the burning mattress. She managed to stand and steady herself, then shuffle to the door. When she reached to open it she couldn't, there was no handle or doorknob. Pushing didn't work. Neither did pulling on the edge. She hammered on the door with her left fist and tried to call out, but her voice was very weak. Smoke stung her eyes and hampered her breathing. She thought of breaking a skylight, picking up something and throwing it at the glass – she even managed to pull the dirty cloth away from one pane. There were bricks lying in a corner, but she had scarcely the strength to pick one up, let alone throw it. She was not aware at that point how badly injured she was, how loss of blood had weakened her.

She put the rag from the skylight to her nose and mouth as a barrier to the stinging smoke. She knew she was sure to burn to death if she didn't get out of that room or smother the flames, but most of her energy had left her. Vaguely she realized she had fallen and was lying on the edge of the burning mattress.

She heard bumping from the direction of the door. The air within the room changed. A man's voice said, 'The door's open.'

Merlyn rallied and, not knowing who the voice belonged to, she got to her feet and steadied herself. As she made it to the door she could hear the man's footsteps running down the stairs. She called to him, begging him to help her.

'I'm passing out... Please...'

'Just keep coming down the stairs!' he called back.

Walking at that point seemed impossible; she had neither the strength nor the coordination. Behind her the attic room was seriously ablaze now. She eased herself down until she was sitting on the top stair. By pulling on the uprights of the banister, she began bumping herself down the stairs. It seemed to take an age, but finally she caught a shaft of light from the open front door below. She dragged herself to her feet again, believing she had to get down much faster, sure that if she didn't the man who had done this to her would jump out and catch her again. Step by precarious step she got herself down more stairs until she could see the open doorway.

Descending the last few feet, she felt the cold air sharpen the pain of her lacerations and burns. In the narrow hallway she had to plough her way through bags and boxes of rubbish and rags, rolling from one wall to the other until finally she made it to the door.

Outside, she could see people, fifty or sixty feet away, standing at a bus stop. They were hazy shapes rather than solid images; her eyes were not focusing as they should. She limped on to the top step and held out her arms.

'Please help me!' she cried. 'I've been raped!'

She leaned against the concrete pillar, exhausted, realizing that no one had heard her, or wanted to hear her. When she called out she had caused some movement, but the shapes at the bus stop still had their backs to her. She was sure people going by had looked across, but they looked away again and kept moving. They stayed uninvolved. Having neither the will nor the strength to do anything else, Merlyn sat down. She put her elbows on her knees so that her hands could prop her chin. After a time she heard sounds that were nearer and more distinct than the others; when she looked she saw yellow hats bobbing towards her on the other side of the railings separating the houses from the road. The fire brigade, she realized. She began thanking them in a hoarse whisper, over and over.

The first fireman to reach her noticed how badly she was bleeding from the wounds on the back of her neck. He called for dressings to be brought; when they came, he applied them and yelled for more. The first constable on the scene covered Merlyn's freezing body and tried to make her comfortable. The fireman was now holding the neck dressings firmly in place, his grip like a tight collar stanching the haemorrhage. Merlyn would learn later that her injuries were so severe that at first sight of her, the fire crew assumed she had been in an explosion.

Two police officers, a sergeant and the constable, were at her side. She told them who she was and that she had been on her way to work when she was waylaid; she gave the best description she could of the man who attacked her.

Somebody shouted: 'Where's that bloody ambulance?' It had been twenty minutes since the call went through, and there was still no sign. Someone else said, more quietly: 'We can't wait any longer. She won't make it.'

They decided to take Merlyn to hospital in the police patrol car. She was lifted with great care and carried to the vehicle, but when the back door was opened they couldn't get her inside, because the fireman didn't want to ease up the pressure on her neck for even a few seconds. The opposite door was opened, and someone clambered into the back seat to ease Merlyn inside. At that moment the ambulance showed up.

Now the procedures became more urgent. There were angry voices, too, one of them shouting at the ambulance crew that they had been called twenty-five minutes ago. Somebody in the ambulance shouted back: there had been a computer breakdown. 'We've only known about this for five minutes!'

The constable was urging Merlyn to stay awake, to hold up. She was put on a stretcher, covered with a blanket and wheeled to the ambulance.

The police officer in charge of the eventual enquiry was Detective Superintendent John Jones. He arrived at the scene as Merlyn was being taken to the ambulance, and he recalled the upset of seeing the condition she was in. 'It was the most traumatic shock,' he said, 'not just to me but to all of us, because certainly in all of my service – and I was a police officer for thirty-four years – the only time I've seen injuries approaching the gravity of these particular ones have been on people who were dead.'

In the ambulance a support dressing was fixed to Merlyn's neck, a drip was set up and an oxygen mask fitted to her face. They set off with sirens blaring, heading for King's College Hospital. Merlyn asked if she still had her rings. A voice said yes, but later she would find two of her three rings had gone – one a silver ring of very little value, the other her mother's wedding ring, the only memento of her Merlyn had possessed.

Detective Constable Mark Chapman was the first CID officer on the scene. When he first saw Merlyn she was sitting on the step. 'No clothes on,' he said. 'Blood everywhere. She was completely white, because she'd lost so much blood. We thought it was a murder investigation.'

At that point DC Chapman was told he would be the exhibits officer for the enquiry. Merlyn was taken off to hospital and the crime scene was sealed. When the forensic team arrived, they went into the house accompanied by Detective Superintendent Jones and DC Chapman. The first task was to make a thorough reconnaissance of the place and to determine the route Merlyn had taken to come down. Next, they examined the room where she was attacked, then photographed it, recording every inch of the place as they found it. When the photography was complete, a search for exhibits began, these being the potential clues – many of them fragmentary, some no more than stains and vague marks – that might add up to a coherent picture of what had been done in there, and perhaps even reveal who did it. Several days of searching would produce 150 exhibits.

DC Chapman's assessment of the house was unequivocal. 'An absolute shit hole,' he said. 'It was a squat. You go in and there's no carpet on the floor. All the rooms are squats. There didn't appear to be anyone else living in the place, but what you've got at the top is bags and bags of rubbish that line the walls. And bottles, Lucozade bottles, Coke bottles, filled with urine – the place stinks. It's absolutely disgusting. You've got syringes, you've got crack pipes, crack bottles, everything in there... most of it's filled with bags of crap. Awful. You get to the top of the stairs and the only room you can get into is the one where Merlyn was attacked. There's no door handle, and when you go in there, all you've got is a mattress. And all these urine bottles and Coke bottles, all surrounding the bed. It was just a complete and utter shit hole.'

At Brixton Police Station Detective Superintendent John Jones set up an incident room and assigned Detective Inspector Hamish Brown to the day-to-day running of the case. Fourteen officers were appropriated from other duties to carry out a round-the-clock investigation. Because facilities at Brixton were seriously overstretched, no computers were available to use on the case: all records would have to be prepared manually and filed the old-fashioned way, in folders, drawers and file boxes.

The investigating team had practically no evidence to work on. All they knew so far was that Merlyn's attacker was black with a flat top haircut, he wore a distinctive blue tracksuit, and he was probably a drug user. They also knew that the place where the attack took place was a squat and a crack house; that was more of a hindrance than a help to the investigation, however, since it meant that countless itinerants as well as most of the crack users in Brixton had used the place at one time or another. It was believed likely that a casual user of the house had set Merlyn free.

By the time the first meeting in the incident room broke up, it had been decided that known drug dealers and users in Brixton would be vigorously questioned, and that door-to-door enquiries would be carried out in the region of Effra Road. Progress meetings would be held in the incident room at four o'clock every day. Detective Superintendent Jones reminded the team that this could still turn into a murder enquiry.

Because of the fire in the attic at Effra Road, then a drenching from fire brigade hoses, much if not all of the potential DNA evidence from exhibits was likely to have been destroyed or seriously degraded. Nevertheless, sixty-five exhibits were sent for DNA testing, eight of them earmarked for the PCR process. PCR stands for polymerase chain reaction, which is a method for repeatedly copying and amplifying the two strands of DNA of a particular gene sequence, so that enough of a scarce sample can be produced to make analysis possible. In the United Kingdom the work is carried out in one laboratory only, at Chepstow, in Gwent. PCR is much faster than DNA testing, though less conclusive, but there is a permanent backlog of samples to be processed at Chepstow, all of them classified as urgent. The samples from Effra Road had to get in the queue. In total, the DNA and PCR tests would take thirteen weeks. All would draw blanks.

Merlyn, meanwhile, having arrived at King's College Hospital at 8.15 a.m., was found to have lost more than four pints of blood. Her condition was critical, and her chances for survival were uncertain. Two blood transfusion lines were set up and support blocks placed around her head to keep it stable while her brain was scanned.

At 9.30 a.m. Merlyn's sister Sharon was telephoned at work by her au pair, who told her the police were on their way to talk to her. When they arrived they took Sharon to a private room and asked her to sit down. Her sister Merlyn, they told her, had been mugged – or, rather, she had been stabbed. No, raped. Well, a man had stabbed and raped her, although it could have been two men. Thus confused and horrified, Sharon naturally broke down. When she had composed herself, the police took her to King's College Hospital in their patrol car. She was met at the hospital by Dr Ruth Brown, who had set up the blood transfusion lines when Merlyn was brought in. Dr Brown took Sharon to a quiet room, where she was given tea and provided with access to a telephone.

Following scanning and radiography, Merlyn was taken back to a cubicle in A&E, still naked under a foil sheet. Shortly afterwards a police forensic technician arrived and proceeded to take swabs. When the procedure was over and he had gone, Sharon came in. Nothing could have prepared her for that first sight of her sister, lying there virtually unrecognizable – and no one had told her that quite apart from having been raped, garrotted and stabbed, Merlyn had been burned. It was difficult for Merlyn to talk because of her injuries, but she wanted people with her and to talk to her sister as much as she could, although Sharon later told her that her voice had been nothing but a whisper.

In the middle of the afternoon WPC Nicola Holding arrived to question Merlyn. This officer had undergone SOIT (Sexual Offences Investigation Techniques) training and was attached to Brixton's Rape Squad; for the duration of the police investigation she would be Merlyn's liaison officer.

At that first meeting, out of sympathy for Merlyn's condition, WPC Holding kept the questioning brief and cursory, recording only an outline of what had happened. Even so, because of her shock at the sight of the injuries and the awfulness of Merlyn's story, Nicola left A&E looking so distressed that a nurse in the corridor asked if she was all right. Nicola admitted she felt faint; the nurse suggested she sit down for a couple of minutes and directed her to a chair a few yards away. Nicola passed out before she could reach it.

For the rest of the day, until Merlyn's blood levels were stabilized and it was time for her to go to surgery, Sharon sat holding her hand, in silence for the most part, simply being the reassuring, loving presence her sister needed.

Merlyn was in theatre for two hours, during which time the surgical team performed repair operations on her throat, neck and hand. Internally, she received 300 stitches to the throat and neck and a hundred externally; her hand needed twenty stitches.

The following day Merlyn was interviewed again, at length this time, by WPC Nicola Holding and another policewoman. A rough sketch was made of the attacker, although Merlyn had serious difficulty in remembering anything about the man's face, apart from his haircut and his bulging eyes. Her recollection of his tracksuit was good, however, so the eventual photofit was comprehensively detailed. It took two days to put together a detailed statement of what had happened in the attic room at 9 Effra Road. It was an exhausting and dispiriting experience for Merlyn and for the police officers, particularly for WPC Holding, who began having nightmares about the attack shortly after she filed the statement.

Meanwhile, the search was on for a duplicate of the attacker's tracksuit. Many designs came to light, all subtly different from each other. A lot of counterfeits turned up too. The police approached retail and distribution outlets, but an exact match eluded them. When DC Mark Chapman contacted Hummel, the Danish company who manufactured the suit, they told him that the design described by Merlyn was one of a limited edition of 5,000 made for Tottenham Hotspur football club. Production had stopped three years before the crime was committed.

A few days after headline reports of the attack appeared in the press, a young woman walked into Brixton Police Station, waited until there was nobody but the desk officer around, then asked him curtly about the sexual act that was carried out on Merlyn: 'Was it something to do with buggery?' The officer told her to wait while he found someone connected with the case, but when he came back she had gone.

On 25 February the police carried out a reconstruction of Merlyn's movements from her flat in Tulse Hill to Effra Road on the morning of the attack. For the purposes of the reconstruction Merlyn was played by her best friend Valerie, who strongly resembled her. Police officers followed Valerie, questioning members of the public and handing out leaflets designed to jog their memories.

After seeing the reconstruction, a bakery delivery driver came forward and told police that on the morning of the attack he parked his van near number 9 Effra Road. At approximately 7.15 a.m. he looked up the steps and saw a white woman and a black man. They stood close together, the man holding the woman's arm. To the witness they appeared to be quarrelling, and he assumed it was a lovers' tiff. He hadn't given the matter another thought until he read the details on the police handout.

As the investigation moved forward, the list of suspects grew. During late February and early March, seventeen men were interviewed and had their homes searched. No charges were brought against any of them. Merlyn, in the meantime, had moved out of her Tulse Hill flat. She had also gone back to hospital to have her stitches removed, and had now flown to Spain to spend a recuperative holiday with her sisters.

A *Crimewatch* appeal was screened by the BBC in the middle of March. As always with these appeals, the case had been picked among others on the basis of the probability that *Crimewatch* viewers might be able to help. The reconstructed incident was delivered sensitively and accurately but without dramatic artifice, presenting the case with clarity and inviting responses from viewers who might know something that would help the police. Remarking on his own feelings about publicity for police investigations, Superintendent Jones said: 'I was always a great believer in using the media, particularly in these kind of cases, because at the end of the day it was always the public who were going to help us.'

Following the *Crimewatch* transmission, twenty-five telephone calls were made to the studio and a further ten to the Brixton incident room. Every call was followed up, but no leads were established. The *Crimewatch* piece, however, prompted a tip-off from a woman called Jeanette, whose black boyfriend was called Tony Ferrira. They had watched *Crimewatch* at home, and at a certain point Jeanette had gone into the bedroom, leaving Ferrira alone watching the programme. When Jeanette came back minutes later, she noticed that Tony looked strange. She asked him if he felt all right. He didn't look up. 'I think I've just seen myself on TV,' he said. Some time later he went to the bathroom and swallowed twenty-five of Jeanette's sleeping pills. She found him apparently asleep on the bed, and she only realized he had taken an overdose when she found the empty bottle lying in the bathroom. She called an ambulance and Ferrira was taken to hospital, where his stomach was washed out. He later discharged himself, refusing to remain under observation. From then on he behaved secretively and his behaviour underwent a number of changes, among them the practice of sleeping out on the roof at night in a sleeping bag. All this deepened Jeanette's suspicions about his reason for trying to kill himself.

A few days after the overdose incident Jeanette rang Brixton Police Station and asked to speak to someone connected with the Merlyn Nuttall case. She was eventually connected with DC Peter 'Jumbo' Redford, and they arranged to meet at Streatham Common. As they talked later, Jeanette identified herself to DC Redford as the woman who had called at the station with the query about buggery in the Nuttall case. She told Redford she was convinced Tony Ferrira was the man they were looking for.

'I'll tell you just what it was he did to her,' she said. 'He always wants to do the same thing to a woman when he's been on crack.'

She was as good as her word and DC Redford was convinced: Ferrira was their man. He told Jeanette she would have to make a statement.

'Not a chance,' she said. 'You know all you need to know – and it wasn't me that told you.'

Back at the incident room, DC Redford found that Tony Ferrira's name had come up before, as a frequenter of the crack house on Effra Road. His record revealed he was twenty-seven years old and had a string of previous convictions for robbery, GBH, burglary, malicious wounding and sexual assault on an thirteen-year-old girl. In prison he had killed another inmate with a pair of scissors and was handed a four-year sentence for manslaughter. He was currently on bail for possession of class-A drugs. DI Hamish Brown decided it would be well worthwhile pulling in Tony Ferrira for questioning. His bail address was the home of another girlfriend, Heidi, but DC Redford said it was likely he would be found at Jeanette's place. DI Brown decided they should raid both women's homes at the same time. That way there would be no suspicion that the tip-off had come from Jeanette, and there was also the off-chance that Ferrira would be with Heidi.

At five o'clock in the morning of 26 March, four unmarked police cars pulled into the car park behind a block of flats in Streatham Hill. Eight officers, led by DI Brown, went quietly to the door of Jeanette's flat and broke it down. They found her in bed with Ferrira. He was pulled naked from the sheets, read his rights, given clothes and driven to Brixton Police Station for questioning. When he was asked why his name appeared on a list of people known to frequent number 9 Effra Road, he refused to comment.

Police searched Jeanette's flat for any clues tying Ferrira to the attack on Merlyn – in particular her handbag, her Shelly shoes and her mother's wedding ring. They were also looking for the Hummel tracksuit. WPC Holding, who was one of the raiding team, found Ferrira's Leeds Building Society passbook, with an entry dated 18 February, the day Merlyn was attacked. WPC Holding went to the Leeds Building Society in Streatham Hill as soon as it opened that morning; she wanted to know everything that had happened there on 18 February, however insignificant. When Jeanette was asked about the possible whereabouts of the Hummel tracksuit, she said she knew nothing about it. She suggested they ask Ferrira's other girlfriend. Heidi's place in West Norwood was already being searched, of course, and there the officers found a Polaroid of Ferrira wearing the Hummel tracksuit.

WPC Holding's enquiries at the building society revealed that Ferrira had been there on 18 February and could be picked out clearly on the tape from the branch CCTV camera. On 28 February Ferrira had revisited the branch and acted aggressively because, he said, a mistake had been made in his passbook entry. In view of Ferrira's agitated behaviour, the branch manager had pressed the video button to catch his image as he stood at the counter. The police now had printouts from both these visits to the branch. On the picture taken on the day Merlyn was attacked, Ferrira clearly had a flat top haircut, but on the second shot, taken ten days later, his hair was cropped and the flat top was gone.

Back at Brixton Police Station, Ferrira continued saying: 'No comment' to all other questions. This continued throughout a number of sessions. The implication was that Ferrira was in control. He now simply refused to speak at all and just stared at the police. Attempts to unsettle him had no effect.

'He exercised his right of silence,' said DI Brown. 'That is, he said absolutely nothing during the interview. I thought I had nothing to lose, and I'd try and get a reaction from him. I confronted him with the pictures of Merlyn when she was taken into hospital, quite awful pictures of her with her throat cut open, and all I got from Ferrira was one stare after another. No other reaction.'

Merlyn flew back from Spain on the evening of 26 March especially to attend an identity parade scheduled for the following day. The parade was held in a special viewing room with a one-way window; on the other side the line-up of men stood against a wall, each with a number in front of him. Merlyn was nervous, even though her sister Sharon was with her, and the longer she was kept waiting the more edgy she became. In the viewing chamber with them were police officers and another woman identified to Merlyn as the suspect's solicitor. In preparing for the parade Ferrira had exercised his right to choose nine out of a possible fifteen candidates for the line-up; since he was also entitled to have everyone change their clothing, he exercised that right too. Wearing old clothes and with his hair longer and differently styled, he told the supervising officer he was ready to go ahead with the parade.

After listening to instructions on how to make her decision, Merlyn moved slowly along the line, twice, invisible to the men on the other side of the window. Merlyn was at a huge disadvantage because Ferrira had been able to alter his appearance dramatically. She wavered between number seven and three and finally identified number three as her attacker. Ferrira was number seven.

The investigating officers were devastated. A positive ID had been their only hope of collaring Ferrira. 'People were inconsolable,' said DI Brown. 'Not angry, because Merlyn had done her best.'

Ferrira was kept at the police station for the full ninety hours permitted by law. DI Brown called Jeanette to the station and tried to persuade her to make a statement that would give the police a reason to hang on to their prisoner, but she flatly refused. Ferrira was finally released without charge.

WPC Holding visited Merlyn at home a few hours after the ID parade. Merlyn was still deeply upset at the way she had let everyone down. WPC Holding told her that wasn't so, that people often made wrong identifications; there were so many hazards built into the rules, and it was amazingly simple for someone to change his appearance. She then asked if Merlyn could help her with the search that was still going on for the tracksuit; she held up the Polaroid picture found at Heidi's place. 'Did it look like this?' The picture showed Ferrira, with dreadlocks, sitting by Jeanette's son.

As Merlyn stared at the picture she turned pale. She recognized the eyes. She would never forget them; they were printed on her memory. 'This is the man who attacked me.'

The police had simply wanted a positive identification of the tracksuit, and now they had the identification they had so badly wanted. This development was entirely unexpected, but it was too late and it changed nothing. Ferrira was still free.

Merlyn went back to Spain the following day. Following the ID parade, the investigation wound down and became little more than a routine tying-up of loose ends. Forensic teams were still going through the laborious, time-devouring business of sifting and analysing the material evidence; DI Brown returned to his permanent post at Paddington Green, and the incident room was trimmed to minimal staffing.

On 1 April Ferrira and Jeanette went to a nightclub and left at about one in the morning, Ferrira having drunk a good deal. As the pair walked along the pavement, Jeanette saw two black men coming towards them. As they drew level, one of them said: 'This is for the girl.' They picked up Ferrira by the armpits and threw him through a plate-glass window. Jeanette started screaming, and the men ran off in opposite directions. Eventually, an ambulance was called, and Ferrira was taken away with minor cuts. At the hospital he refused help, assaulted a nurse, and walked out.

Towards the end of April, by which time the investigation was treading water, forensic technicians at a police laboratory made an unforeseen discovery. While examining a bloodstained serviette from the Effra Road crime scene, they found a partial fingerprint alongside the bloodstains. The print was lifted by a painstaking chemical process and was thereafter identified as belonging to Tony Ferrira. The blood on the serviette was Merlyn's.

The police discussed this new evidence with the Crown Prosecution Service (CPS), who saw problems. The fingerprint did no more than place Ferrira at the scene of the crime. Had the print been *mingled* with the blood, it would have argued for Merlyn and Ferrira being in the crack house at the same time; as the evidence stood, it could be used only to show that Ferrira dropped a serviette in the house, and at some point Merlyn chanced to bleed on it. The other evidence in the case was similarly thin, and Merlyn's failure to pick out Ferrira at the ID parade had done nothing to help. The police were nevertheless convinced that Ferrira was the guilty party, and their certainty persuaded the CPS that there was a case to answer. Superintendent Jones was told he could charge Ferrira. At the same time he was advised to use the time Ferrira was on remand to come up with stronger evidence.

On 1 May Ferrira was arrested and charged with the attempted murder of Merlyn Nuttall. At the committal hearing, his trial was set to commence on 19 October 1992 at the Old Bailey. He was charged on the basis of three clues only: the picture of himself wearing the

Hummel tracksuit, the fingerprint on the bloodstained serviette, and the CCTV evidence showing that on the day of the assault he had sported a flat-top haircut, just as Merlyn had claimed in her description of him. These clues were the bare minimum with which a charge could be brought.

In the event of grevious bodily harm with intent being offered, Merlyn was asked how she would feel about it. She pointed out that Ferrira had tried to murder her and he should be tried for the crime he had committed, for the grotesque things he had done. The charge of attempted murder stood.

Throughout the period leading up to the trial date, DI Brown and WPC Holding kept in touch with Ferrira's girlfriends, Jeanette and Heidi. They visited them regularly, trying to wear them down and persuade them to make statements that would put backbone in the prosecution case. But the women doggedly refused. They did not like what their man had done, but a misplaced loyalty to Ferrira, plus an undisguised fear of him, provided all the determination they needed – they would not officially say a word against him.

Through prison sources the police learned that Ferrira could reach out to the women from remand, and he was exercising some pressure to keep them in line. However, the regular visits from the police did start to wear Jeanette down, and one night she gave them some new information. She said that on the night of 17–18 February they had had a row and he walked out at about eleven o'clock in the evening. Jeanette said she didn't see him again until nine o'clock the next morning. He had let himself into the flat, and when he entered the bedroom he was completely naked. Jeanette asked him where his clothes were. He said he had committed an aggravated burglary at East Dulwich and his clothes had been soiled in the raid, so as soon as he got back he had put them in the rubbish bin outside the flat. Jeanette noticed that his breathing was oddly laboured and that his face was scratched. When he had showered and put on fresh clothes, he went out again. Two hours later, when he returned, his hair had been shaved off on top. When she was asked what clothes Ferrira had worn when he went out on the evening of 17 February, Jeanette said: 'It was that Hummel tracksuit you keep on about.' So the tracksuit had been dumped and was presumably buried in the landfill site at Mucking, in Essex, where all of Streatham's refuse is taken.

Six police officers were assigned to scour the dump. They were looking for the tracksuit, possibly Merlyn's handbag, the missing ring and her shoes. Working in overalls, gloves and masks, and aided by four council refuse workers, plus a digger, a dumper and a Land Rover, they spent two weeks sifting the rubbish at a cost of £15,000. They found nothing.

Around this time, funds ran so low that the incident room was closed. WPC Holding continued to work on the case in her own time with help from DC Chapman. One evening, when they were talking to Heidi at her flat in Norwood, she admitted that on the Monday night before the attack on Merlyn, at some time after eleven o'clock, Ferrira showed up at her place wearing the Hummel tracksuit. She said he stayed with her until just after six o'clock on Tuesday morning, then he called a cab.

A cab? This was bombshell news for the police. Had Heidi any idea what cab company he had used? Of course, she said, it was the one they always used; the number was on the pad by the phone.

Within a very short time the taxi firm's logged early-morning bookings for 18 February were checked, the appropriate one traced and the driver located. His name was Steve Duggan, and he told the police he had expected them a lot sooner. Yes, when the case broke in the papers he had realized the possible involvement of his fare that morning. But with his wife pregnant and his occupation dangerous enough as it was, Duggan wanted no trouble if he could avoid it. He apologized for not coming forward voluntarily.

His signed statement, made later that day at Brixton Police Station, declared that at 6.20 a.m. on Tuesday 18 February 1992 he picked up a West Indian man at a flat in West Norwood and drove him to Effra Road in Brixton, as requested. On the way the passenger asked Duggan to stop for a few minutes while he got out and visited a house well known to cab drivers as an address where drugs could be bought. When eventually they drew up in Effra Road, the passenger told Duggan to wait again while he went inside to get the fare money from a friend. The passenger then ducked through railings that separated a row of houses from the main road. After ten minutes the passenger still hadn't reappeared. Duggan realized he wasn't coming back, so he left.

Because of this new evidence, the trial date was put back to 11 January 1993.

Meanwhile, Jeanette and Heidi remained entrenched. In spite of the valuable help they had given the police, neither of them would yet officially 'grass up' Tony Ferrira. Argument and cajolery seemed to have no effect; the women were staying off the record.

WPC Nicola Holding was prepared to believe they would never budge, but she also believed she had a duty to keep trying to persuade them, and patient moralizing finally paid off. Steadily reminding Jeanette that the man she protected so stubbornly was viciously subhuman and a menace to women, that he had done untold damage to one innocent woman already, and that given the freedom he would do it again, WPC Holding finally prevailed on Jeanette to give evidence for the prosecution. When Heidi was told what Jeanette was prepared to do, she relented and said she, too, would speak for the prosecution.

At a stroke, the police had solid witnesses. By providing information about Ferrira's movements and the clothing he wore during the crucial hours on 17 and 18 February, the women could seriously strengthen the police case and undermine whatever credibility Tony Ferrira might have.

Between the time she made her statement and the opening of the trial, Jeanette was approached in the street by a black man who ran his finger down her cheek, miming a knife stroke. She understood well enough what she was being told. At approximately the same time, Ferrira called Heidi from prison and warned her not to start saying the wrong things to anybody. It was hard for the police to know just how seriously the threats had damaged the women's resolve. With luck, of course, intimidation might harden their hearts against Ferrira and make them more determined to put him away.

The trial began at the Old Bailey on Monday 11 January 1993. By then, DI Brown and the prosecuting counsel, John Nutting, were uneasy about calling Jeanette as a witness. Recent bouts of moodiness and reticence suggested problems ahead: she might either retract her statement or tell the court that she had made it under duress. A hostile witness was the last thing the prosecution needed. The eventual decision to go ahead and call Jeanette was made only twenty minutes before the trial began.

Merlyn gave lucid, painfully detailed evidence to the court, and it clearly shook a number of those present in the public gallery and on the jury benches. When Jeanette's turn came she was a flawless witness, delivering her evidence crisply and sticking to it in spite of defence attempts to rattle her. Heidi's account of Ferrira's movements meshed perfectly with Jeanette's testimony. Taken as a whole, the depositions of Jeanette, Heidi and taxi driver Duggan amounted to a reinforcement of Merlyn's story and pointed strongly to Ferrira's guilt. The woman also testified that Ferrira had requested from them the same unusual sexual act as he had with Merlyn. Circumstantial evidence is often too fragile to withstand rebuttal, but the interlocking testimonies of these witnesses overwhelmed the defence case.

The trial lasted eight days, at the end of which the jury, having been out for two hours, found Tony Ferrira guilty. Judge Lowry, presiding, sentenced the accused to five years for kidnap, eight years for indecent assault and twenty years for attempted murder, the sentences to run concurrently.

In the aftermath of her ordeal, Merlyn Nuttall has become much more than a survivor. Toughened in mind and spirit, she has purposely put the past where it belongs.

Today Merlyn is confident, fulfilled and happily married. She has her own successful fashion business, and in 1998 she was voted *Cosmopolitan* Woman of Achievement. She sits on the Sexual Offences Advisory Group that was set up by the Metropolitan Police and she helped to launch Haven, a 24-hour dedicated rape centre based at King's College, London. She also works closely with Victim Support as a spokesperson and adviser on victims' needs. She has shown incredible courage and no resentments wound her. In her own words, she has blanked Ferrira from her emotions, and he evokes neither hatred nor forgiveness in her.

This chapter is partly based on the book *It Could Have Been You* by Merlyn Nuttall and Sharon Morrison, Virago (1997).

plymouth attack

In November 1997 Mrs Joan Cavendish, a 59-year-old antique dealer, fell and suffered a serious head wound while she was working in her shop in Plymouth. That, at any rate, was what appeared to have happened.

Mrs Cavendish's son Shaun was contacted in New York and came home as soon as he could, arriving three days after his mother was admitted to hospital. He learned that a friend of hers, a local businessman, had gone into the antique shop at about 12.20 p.m. on Wednesday 26 November and found Mrs Cavendish lying behind the counter. He assumed she had fainted and struck her forehead on the counter as she fell. He called an ambulance, and Mrs Cavendish was taken to nearby Derriford Hospital. Her head wound needed seven stitches, but the underlying damage was more serious: she had suffered a cerebral haemorrhage and remained unconscious for a considerable time. When she did come round she had no recollection of what had happened. She assumed, as her friend did, that she had passed out and struck her head as she went down

After spending some time at his mother's bedside, Shaun went to the shop to tidy up and make sure everything was secure. While he was there, for no reason other than curiosity, he rewound the shop's CCTV tape and took it back with him to his mother's house.

That evening he viewed it. Following some mundane footage where very little happened, he saw a man enter the shop and browse near the counter. Mrs Cavendish then appeared, and the man took something – it looked like a ring box – from a Next carrier bag and put it on the counter, drawing her attention to it. As she picked it up and looked at it he suddenly pulled a cylindrical weapon from the bag and hit her on the head with it. Mrs Cavendish fell back, and the man proceeded to burgle the shop. The image on the tape was not clear enough to show the man's facial features.

Shaun was horrified to see this and called in the police. When they had watched the video they visited the shop and carried out a preliminary inspection. While they were there they found the ring box the robber had produced – it was lying behind the counter. It had been taped shut, probably to give the man time to pull the weapon from the bag. The weapon itself was later estimated to be a foot long by about two inches in diameter. It was never found.

The police realized that the trail had been cooling for several days before they were alerted. A HOLMES incident room was set up with DI Chris Carter in charge. DC Simon Blackshire and DC Derek Farrow set about tracing, investigating and eliminating local men with previous convictions for robbery, while DC Gerry Rogers was assigned as Family Liaison Officer. As well as checking potential suspects, DCs Farrow and Blackshire also searched every locker in the bus station, since it was possible that the attack on Mrs Cavendish was the work of a travelling criminal – Plymouth is often visited by that kind of traveller. In the meantime, the police were having the tape from the antique shop's CCTV electronically enhanced to try to produce a better likeness of the attacker. All that seemed certain about him, so far, was that he was left-handed: he had landed the blow to his victim's head using his left hand, and as he robbed the drawers and cabinets after the attack, his left hand was dominant throughout.

As Mrs Cavendish began showing signs of deep-seated neurological damage, her doctors admitted that her condition was giving cause for concern. The police knew that soon they might be handling a murder enquiry. The pace of the investigation was stepped up. Images of the attacker were circulated internally within the Devon and Cornwall Police, then regional newspapers and television were contacted and brought in on the investigation. Early responses produced a number of suspects, but they were all quickly eliminated. As the lines of enquiry began to peter out as fast as they were generated, a decision was made to approach *Crimewatch*.

An appeal was eventually broadcast on the programme on 27 January 1998, during which CCTV footage of Mrs Cavendish being attacked was seen by millions of viewers. Of the calls made in response to the programme, two named the same man. The more specific of the two claimed that the appearance of the robber on the video, as well as the circumstances of the crime, fitted a thirty-year-old man called Glenn Evans, who had been living in Hanover Road in Plymouth at the time of the attack, but had now moved to Stoke-on-Trent. The anonymous caller gave Evans' address in both places.

The following day DCs Blackshire and Farrow visited Evans' old address in Plymouth. The landlord confirmed that Evans and his girlfriend had lived there in November and December the previous year. In the now-empty room they found a Next carrier bag like the one carried by the attacker in the video – no forensic evidence was obtained from this find. According to the landlord, Evans tended to be withdrawn and quiet. His girlfriend Victoria appeared to do all the talking. When neighbours were questioned about the couple, they said they had the impression that Evans had been in the area looking for work; Victoria was still married to another man, and she still visited her in-laws, which apparently caused friction between her and Evans. The neighbours were shown a clip from the CCTV; every one of them agreed that the attacker bore a resemblance to Evans. When the Police National Computer record was checked, it showed that Evans had previous convictions, although they were minor.

By now, the officers on the case had looked at the video of the robbery so many times that the attacker's stature, stance and body movements had become very familiar. When DCs Blackshire and Farrow were sent to Stoke-on-Trent with a search warrant, they were pretty certain they would know the real villain if they came across him.

'I felt confident that as soon as I saw the offender I would recognize him,' said DC Blackshire. 'And that was the case when we did knock on the door of Evans' address in Stoke-on-Trent.'

They arrived at 7 a.m., being more likely to find Evans at home at such an hour. They were accompanied by two officers from the local police station. When they knocked on the door it was Evans who answered. From the instant he stepped into the light, neither of the Plymouth detectives had any doubt: this was who they were after. They showed Evans the warrant and told him why they were there.

Evans said: 'No, it wasn't me. You're welcome to search.'

DC Blackshire asked Evans to sign his pocket book, ostensibly to confirm that he had been cautioned. Evans signed with his left hand. The premises were thoroughly searched, but nothing significant was found. DC Farrow stayed at the house to take Victoria's statement while DC Blackshire and the other two officers took Evans to Stoke Police Station to process his details. Victoria was unhelpful. She told DC Farrow she knew of no robbery, or of any unusual behaviour on Glenn Evans' part. As far as she knew, he had been in Plymouth to seek work.

Later that day the detectives took Evans back to Plymouth, where they interviewed him that night in the presence of a solicitor. Evans couldn't be budged. He flatly denied the crime, repeating several times that he had been in Plymouth looking for work, that was all.

The following morning the detectives asked Evans if he would co-operate by taking part in a staged reconstruction at the antique shop. He had the right to refuse, but he agreed to do it, saying that a simple comparison would show that the man in the reconstruction on the second tape would be nothing like the robber on the first. At the antique shop he allowed DC Blackshire to comb back his hair in the style worn by the man on the video. They then went through a reconstruction, filmed on the shop's CCTV system and by a police cameraman using a separate camera. Directed by the detectives, Evans entered the shop, paused and looked into the cabinets, repeating a number of the actions performed by the man on the original tape – which Evans had not yet seen.

When the reconstruction was over, Evans was taken back to the police interview room, where for the first time he was shown the original CCTV footage. He looked surprised by the violence of the attack, and he strongly denied that the man on the screen was him. The taped reconstruction was then played. When it was over, DC Blackshire asked Evans if he still insisted the man in the original tape wasn't him. 'Are you still saying that you were never in that shop before today?'

'That's what I'm saying, yes.'

'Well, I'll tell you this,' said DC Blackshire, 'now we've had a look at both tapes, we're even more certain it was *you* who attacked that lady and then robbed her.'

Blackshire explained what was going to happen now. The tapes were going to be expertly compared under the most meticulously fair conditions. If, in the view of experts, there were points of similarity between the male figures in the two tapes which determined they were in fact the same man, that opinion would be used as the basis of a prosecution.

By that time the police had held Evans for as long as they were permitted by law, and since there was not enough evidence to warrant a charge, he had to be released. They kept his passport, however, which they had taken during the search of his home. When Evans went back to Stoke, so did DCs Blackshire and Farrow because they wanted to make further enquiries.

Their time was not wasted. They discovered that five or six members of Evans' family in Stoke had seen the *Crimewatch* appeal and had spoken to him the following day about his resemblance to the man on the antique shop tape. This information was grudgingly given, but it served to reinforce the officers' conviction that Evans was their man. Another piece of encouraging news at around that time was that Mrs Cavendish's condition was showing signs of improvement.

DC Farrow recalled that it was a time of intensely mixed feelings for himself and his colleague. 'It was both disappointing and challenging... We knew it was him; now we had to prove it. I felt that his girlfriend was certainly somebody who should be spoken to, and that if we spent more time with her, and she realized what he had in actual fact done, then she would have come across with more information.'

So Victoria was interviewed again. This time she was asked if she would look at the original CCTV from the antique shop, then tell the detectives truthfully if she believed it wasn't Glenn Evans she saw attacking Mrs Cavendish.

Victoria thought about it for a moment, then shrugged. 'If it'll make you leave us alone, I don't mind.'

She was taken to the police station and shown the tape. The uninhibited violence of the attack obviously shocked her. Her customary air of self-confidence disappeared, along with her hostility.

'The phone call to *Crimewatch* aside,' said DC Farrow, 'showing the video to Evans' girlfriend was the real key to unlocking the case. Their relationship had been under a bit of strain anyway, and until that point she'd never seen the actual impact of the blow... To tell you the truth, I think it frightened her.'

Victoria began by admitting that she recognized the clothes worn by the man as having belonged to Evans. Then she folded and told the detectives everything she knew. One day in November 1998, she had left their home in Plymouth early to visit relatives. When she got back, some time in the early afternoon, Evans wasn't there. When he did show up a short time after, he was agitated and sweating. He wore several layers of clothing, which made him look rather stout, and he had some kind of plastic make-up or latex on his face. He had gelled his hair, something he had never done before, and it was combed straight back, whereas normally he wore it combed forward. He would not explain what he was up to and he behaved in a thoroughly furtive, jumpy manner. He took a shower, and when he came out of the bathroom he handed Victoria a bagful of clothes, which he told her to dump. Later she saw him sorting out jewellery in envelopes on the bed. Three or four days after that they returned to Stoke-on-Trent. They visited a second-hand shop in Stoke and Evans sold the jewellery there.

DC Blackshire left the interview at that point to follow up the story about the jewellery. While DC Farrow was still interviewing Victoria, Evans himself turned up at the police station. He complained to the desk officer that his girlfriend was being held there against her will and without a solicitor. In fact, he knew no such thing, but had probably guessed she was with the police, and he was worried about what she might be telling them.

DC Farrow went out to the desk to speak to Evans and to explain that Victoria was making a statement of her own free will, and that she was free to leave at any time she chose. As Farrow was talking, his mobile phone rang. He stepped back a pace and answered it. DC Blackshire was on the other end. He had just been to the second-hand shop Victoria had told them about. The friendly owner had not only acknowledged buying the jewellery, but he still had some of it – one piece, a rose gold watch, was in his safe, together with a receipt bearing Evans' signature. The watch would later be identified by Mrs Cavendish.

DC Farrow thanked his colleague and switched off his mobile. He stepped close to Evans and told him that since his release from custody, fresh evidence of his involvement in the Plymouth robbery had come to light. In view of that evidence, Evans was now under arrest.

Later that day Evans was taken back to Plymouth, where, under questioning, he admitted carrying out the attack on Mrs Cavendish. He robbed her, he said, because he needed funds to open a road-side café with his girlfriend. When his case went to court on 14 August 1998, he pleaded guilty to robbery and was sentenced to ten years' imprisonment.

Mrs Cavendish still suffers from her injuries. She has had to give up her shop, and among a number of disabilities she has lost all sense of taste and smell. She has severe vertigo and cannot walk far without the aid of a stick.

murder on
campus

It often happens that crimes which are simple or quick to solve will nevertheless involve the police in time- and budget-consuming searches for suspects before enquiries can move on towards their conclusion. The case study that follows, brief though it is, illustrates how an appeal transmitted on *Crimewatch* can dramatically reduce the time and resources needed to round off an investigation.

On Guy Fawkes Day 1999, Elizabeth Stacey showed up for work as usual at the Regent Campus of the University of Westminster in Regent Street, London. Elizabeth, twenty-four, graduated from Cambridge with a degree in physics and had joined the staff of the University of Westminster two months earlier. She worked as a technician in the psychology department, a post she saw as a preliminary rung on her career ladder. The job required Elizabeth to do a little teaching, but her main work was to use her IT skills – she was *very* good with computers and specialized software – to guide and assist students, as well as help expand the scope of the department's computer network. While she was at Westminster, Elizabeth planned to develop her IT capabilities still further, to a point where she could cross over into the area of environmental physics, where she hoped to make her full-time career.

On that Friday morning she appeared as buoyant as ever, a friendly, slightly shy person who brought drive and endless patience to her work. One of the projects she was involved with at that time was the creation of a departmental website, which she was jointly designing with a postgraduate student called Steven Reid. The first time they were seen together that morning was in the university coffee shop. Elizabeth greeted Reid brightly and asked him how he was. He complained of being tired because of the amount of data he was having to cope with. Elizabeth told him he worried too much; he shouldn't let the work get on top of him. They spoke briefly about a couple of problems with the website, then Elizabeth went off to talk to someone else.

Later that morning, in the postgrad computer room, Elizabeth was helping a student called Gary with a software problem. They had been there a few minutes when Reid came in. He cleared his throat to attract Elizabeth's attention. When she turned he was immediately apologetic, said he was sorry to bother her, but he was having trouble getting into Windows on the computer he was using at the moment – would she mind coming and having a look?

Elizabeth said sure, she was just finishing with Gary, she would be along in a couple of minutes. Reid stayed where he was, frowning. There was an awkward moment. It was obvious to the student that Reid wanted Elizabeth to help him straight away.

'Right now?' she said.

Reid nodded. 'It's just... I can't get on with anything unless...'

'OK.' Elizabeth got up. 'Let's have a look.' She walked out of the room with Reid. At the door she gave Gary a little wave. 'See you later.'

That was the last time anyone reported seeing Elizabeth alive. For the rest of the day she was noticeably absent from the department. People assumed she had gone home – she would presumably have told *somebody* why. That evening she had a prearranged meeting with a friend, but she failed to show up at the rendezvous. Her mother didn't hear from her either.

'We found out on the Friday evening that she was missing and hadn't turned up to meet her friend, and that was worrying,' said her mother, Sheila Stacey. 'It was very unusual for Elizabeth. She nearly always phoned us, so we started worrying then and we went to the police station. They were helpful and phoned round all her friends…'

But although Sheila Stacey was grateful for the trouble the police were taking, her instinct told her this was more than a simple breakdown in communications. 'I really knew in my heart of hearts because, you know, it was so unusual for her not to phone us, that… we knew something was very wrong.'

Police making enquiries at the university established that Elizabeth had last been seen leaving the postgrad computer room with Steven Reid on Friday morning. Reid was now missing too. Since Elizabeth had not shown up at her flat, and she had not been seen leaving work, it was important that the police eliminate the possibility that she was still in the university building. They organized an overnight search, helped by police dogs, but a number of rooms were locked and several of the key-holders could not be contacted. On Saturday morning, while police officers were in the university security room viewing CCTV tapes, a psychology technician, one of Elizabeth's colleagues, managed to get a key to a locked room on an upper floor. He went to the room, opened it and found Elizabeth inside. She was dead. She had head injuries, and there were signs of a violent struggle. The technician ran downstairs to tell the police.

Both Detective Chief Inspector Guy Ferguson and Detective Sergeant John McFarlane were watching the Rugby World Cup at their separate homes when their pagers alerted them that the body had been discovered. Ferguson got to the university building as soon as he could and found McFarlane already there. The scene where Elizabeth's body lay had been secured. The DCI quickly got himself up to date on what was known and tasked the forensic team. It appeared that Elizabeth had been killed by several blows to the side of the head with a blunt instrument, and there were signs that she had put up a considerable struggle.

'She was last seen with Steven Reid, a postgraduate student who also works here as a technician,' DS McFarlane reported. 'That was yesterday morning, and there's been no sign of him since.' The opinion around the campus, DS McFarlane added, was that Reid, a Scot, was definitely a loner and people knew very little about him.

'Have we got his address?'

'Yes, sir.'

DCI Ferguson sent a team round to Reid's flat to search the place for indications of where he might be, clues to his nature and possible preoccupations, and addresses of relatives and acquaintances. From the very start of the enquiry there was no doubt who the police needed to talk to. Reid's disappearance at or near the time Elizabeth Stacey died automatically qualified him for priority investigation.

'Either he was another victim of the offence,' said DS McFarlane, 'or alternatively he was involved in the assault on her.'

It was important to find Reid, but in the meantime it was just as critical to obtain a reliable profile of the man and an idea of his probable moves. If he was alive, and if he had killed Elizabeth, then the police had to know the kind of individual they were dealing with.

'At the very least he was going to be a significant witness to the enquiry,' DCI Ferguson said. 'Getting hold of him at an early stage was obviously key to our investigation right from the start.'

At Reid's flat the police went through notebooks, diaries, address books and anything else with writing on it. The only fact that emerged with any certainty was that Reid had entertained notions of killing himself. Extensive questioning of staff at the university turned up very little about him, and the scraps that were known about his off-campus life were scarcely revealing. Earlier in the year, for example, he had been in Cornwall to watch the total eclipse of the sun, and while he was there he had stayed in a cottage on the Lizard Peninsula. He had revealed to a couple of staff members that he liked Cornwall, and he said he had a friend living there. His personal university web page produced nothing enlightening either. However, by coincidence, the university was able to provide the police with a good photograph of him that they had taken during university research into facial identification and CCTV.

'We had information that he used to go for long walks on Hampstead Heath,' said DS McFarlane. 'We carried out a search, using dogs and a helicopter, to make sure that he wasn't lying dead on the Heath.'

Officers were sent to check the cottage where Reid had stayed in Cornwall in case he had gone there; while they were in the area they would brief the local police and newspapers. Within a couple of days all mainline railway stations between London and Edinburgh displayed a wanted poster with a picture of Reid and a description – white male, thirty-three years old, six feet tall, slim build, brown/green eyes, short, dark-brown hair longer on top, tanned complexion, Scottish accent. There were a number of reported sightings of him in Edinburgh, which was where he grew up, but the police could find no trace of him there. His mother still lived in the city, and when she was interviewed she became very distressed. She said she had been expecting to see her son quite soon, and indeed police searching his flat had found a train ticket he had bought for the visit.

After a week of intensive investigation there was still no indication of where Reid might be. Television appeals in London and Cornwall failed to raise any significant response.

'I was concerned as time went on that Steven might have tucked himself away somewhere where we'd never find him,' said DCI

Ferguson. 'I was feeling that if he had killed himself immediately afterwards, then we would have found him fairly quickly, because he would have come to light. But once that first few days had passed, then I was thinking more that he had made some effort to conceal himself.'

The detectives now needed to track down Reid as a matter of urgency. They contacted *Crimewatch* with a view to having an appeal broadcast nationwide, and Reid's picture was shown on the programme on Tuesday 16 November. A number of viewers rang the studio and the police incident room to report sightings of Reid along the M5 corridor to Cornwall. One call came from a woman who said she had seen Reid selling the *Big Issue* outside Marks & Spencer on Western Road in Brighton. The following day Brighton police had a call from a woman running a drop-in centre; she said that one of the men using the centre saw the *Crimewatch* piece and recognized Reid as a man who had recently visited the centre. Brighton police telephoned the London detectives and asked for details of Reid's distinguishing features. Armed with the information, two Brighton CID officers and two uniform constables approached the man selling the *Big Issue* on Western Road; they could see straight away that he was the one they were after. When he was asked his name, he said he was Robbie Foster, but after he was taken into custody he admitted he was Steven Reid.

Back in London, he confessed freely to having murdered Elizabeth Stacey, betraying no emotion as he spoke. 'He was very quiet and subdued in interview,' said DS McFarlane. 'He described in great detail the assault on Elizabeth Stacey… He came across as a very selfish individual.'

Reid explained that he had lied about having difficulty getting into Windows on one of the computers, and had asked Elizabeth to help him. A few days earlier he had gone to John Lewis and bought a rolling pin, which he later secreted in the room with the allegedly faulty computer. He had also purchsed adhesive tape which he'd cut into strips and set out in the room, intending to use it as some form of binding. He said that once they were in the room and Elizabeth was preoccupied with the computer, he hit her on the side of the head five or six times with the rolling pin. She collapsed and he pulled her to the corner of the office and tried to hide her. He left her there unconscious, unconcerned whether she was dead or dying, and deliberately locked the door so people couldn't get in.

Reid immediately left the building, being careful first to lock the door again. He took the tube from Oxford Circus to Euston and checked into a run-down hotel in Euston Square for two nights. In his room he swallowed several Anadin tablets in an attempt to kill himself, but he vomited and cleared most of the tablets out of his stomach before they had time to dissolve. He later tried to slash his wrists, but to the police the marks looked like evidence of a half-hearted attempt. While he was in the hotel he saw his photograph on television; he immediately shaved off his moustache. Following another botched suicide attempt with pills he left the hotel and took a bus to Hemel Hempstead. He bought a sleeping bag and more clothes from a second-hand shop and began sleeping rough. He eventually decided to go to Brighton because he believed that it might be warmer there for sleeping outside.

In Brighton he adopted the name of Robbie Foster and made contact with organizations that help the homeless. His cover story was to tell anyone who probed him on his background that he had to leave Scotland in a hurry to get away from a drug dealer. He had been in Brighton only a few days when he was arrested.

If Reid had stayed where he was and simply maintained a low profile, there was no saying how long he might have remained at large. 'Without *Crimewatch*'s help I don't think we'd have found him in Brighton,' said DS McFarlane. 'There were no leads to suggest he was there, no intelligence and no information.'

What the police and colleagues at the University of Westminster wanted to know, most of all, was why Steven Reid, a previously non-violent person, a homely loner, had committed such a crime.

'His explanation,' said DS McFarlane, 'was that he was a lonely man in this life, he'd no real friends. He felt that he wanted to commit suicide and that he didn't want to die alone. He stated that Elizabeth was the nicest person he knew and that he wanted to take her with him.'

On 4 July 2000 Steven Reid was found guilty of manslaughter on the grounds of diminished responsibility, and was sentenced to life imprisonment.

wanted

Reports of attacks on old people invariably arouse public indignation. In the early spring of 1996, in the Welsh town of Barry in the Vale of Glamorgan, the vicious battering of two elderly women shocked the community and sparked an intensive police manhunt.

The first small alarm sounded a few minutes after 8 p.m. on the evening of Wednesday 20 March when Sheila Mounter was telephoned at home in Barry by her cousin Kitty in Worcestershire. Marjorie was worried because ninety-year-old Aunt Enid wasn't answering the phone. Sheila Mounter and her husband Richard lived a short way up the road from the flats where the aunt, Enid Poole, lived alone; they were in regular contact with the old lady and had seen her the previous day. Sheila promised they would check on her right away. As soon as Kitty rang off, Sheila tried twice to call her aunt, but there was no answer. The Mounters then decided it would be best to look in on her, just in case. They walked briskly along to the complex of flats and let themselves in to Enid's place with their own keys. When they walked into the sitting room they found Enid lying on the floor. She appeared to have been cut about the face and head. Her clothes and the carpet around her were soaked with blood. Sheila tried to speak to her, but she was barely conscious.

The sitting room had been ransacked. Drawers had been pulled out and their contents scattered. Ornaments were broken, furniture had been overturned and the phone, which had been connected to the local authority helpline, was ripped out. The rest of the flat had been turned over too, but the sitting room was the worst, with blood over the floor and on the walls.

Sheila Mounter ran to a neighbour's and called the emergency services from the telephone there. In the flat, kneeling by Enid, Richard Mounter realized she was still wearing her day clothes, and the curtains hadn't been drawn. How long had she been lying there? And how had her attacker got in? There was only one door, and it wasn't damaged. If this had been a burglary, it had been an inept one – Richard had already seen cash and jewellery littered around the flat. A likely explanation, the police would say later, was that the intruder was so frenzied that he wasn't capable of systematically burgling the flat.

An ambulance and emergency team arrived just after 8.30 p.m. While the paramedics were attending to Enid, two uniformed police constables arrived. One of them spoke to Enid, who had rallied a little and was looking about her, confused and shocked. He asked her if she had fallen. She said she had, but to the PC the injuries on her face and head looked like nothing caused by a domestic mishap. He put through a call to the station to say that CID officers and Scenes of Crimes Officers would be needed at the scene, as this was clearly an attack, not an accident.

Detective Sergeant Phil Williams arrived just as Enid Poole had been taken on a stretcher to the ambulance. DS Williams paused for a quick briefing from a PC who was taping off the entrance to the flat.

'It's a Mrs Poole,' the PC said. 'She's a very old lady. Somebody wanted to kill her, from the look of it. Niece and niece's husband, called Mounter, are in the wagon with her.'

DS Williams went to the open back doors of the ambulance and introduced himself. He asked what had happened, and Sheila told him all she knew – the battered woman on the stretcher was her aunt Enid, and she and Richard had found her like this on the floor of her sitting room. DS Williams spoke gently to Enid, asking her if she could remember what had happened, but her consciousness was fading again. Williams promised the Mounters that the police would keep in touch, then he stepped back to let the attendant close the ambulance doors. He had been shaken at the sight of such brutal punishment inflicted on an old lady, and he knew from experience how the news of this assault would affect other people in the district.

'The elderly often have a perception that we live in a very violent society, to the extent that they won't go out at night,' he said later, 'and in many cases won't go out in the day, because of the fear of crime. When something like this happens, it tends to reinforce that perception, so it affects the quality of life of a great number of people.'

For the families of victims there is often as much bewilderment as pain. At first Sheila Mounter found herself incredulous. 'I couldn't believe it at the time,' she said. 'But after a few hours I thought, this is terrible. How someone could do this to *anyone*, never mind a ninety-year-old.'

And the Mounters had the added distress of knowing that throughout a seemingly placid, uneventful afternoon and evening, Enid Poole had been lying in her flat in grave need of help. 'It happened about half past three in the afternoon,' Richard said, 'so obviously she'd been lying there for some time – it was about half-past eight before we actually got down there in the evening. What was going through her mind, what she'd attempted to do under those circumstances, we just don't know.'

By 9.25 p.m. door-to-door enquiries had begun around the flats in the complex. The Police Divisional Commander arrived to be briefed on the case and to see the crime scene for himself. Shortly afterwards a floodlit search of the area began. It was arranged that an extensive forensic search of Enid Poole's flat should start first thing the following morning. Meanwhile, Scenes of Crimes Officers went in and swabbed for blood, saliva and any other evidence, before available specimens deteriorated to a point where they could be of no use to the investigation.

At first the police believed that Enid had been the victim of a distraction burglary – that is, she was distracted by some means or other while the burglary took place. Enid probably let in the burglar, who attacked her during the course of the crime. The case was being treated as a potential murder enquiry because Enid's chances of survival were poor. An incident room would be set up immediately at Barry Police Station.

A police surgeon's report on Enid Poole's injuries made pitiful reading. It stated that she had two black eyes with a laceration beneath the right eye, lacerations on her temple and right ear, heavy bruising on her lower lip, chin, shoulders, hands and knees. Subsequent evaluation of Enid's injuries by Professor Bernard Knight, an eminent forensic pathologist based at Cardiff, revealed that bruising on the side of her mouth and chin had been caused by the attacker gripping Enid's chin with fingers and thumb. Her facial bruising had been caused by slapping, and her bruised hands were characteristic defensive injuries seen on victims who put up their hands to protect their heads from heavy blows.

Soon after he arrived at the station the following morning, DS Williams took a call from Mrs Rhona Bennett, another resident at the flats, who told him she believed she had actually directed a man to Enid Poole's flat the previous day. DS Williams told Mrs Bennett that he would come over and speak to her straight away.

At approximately the time Mrs Bennett was on the phone to the police, another resident of the flats, Mrs Wilson, had noticed a bottle of milk on the step of a neighbour, 86-year-old Mair Lougher. That was unusual, as Mair usually took in the milk much earlier each day. Mrs

Wilson called on a nearby friend, Mrs Cuthbert, and told her about the milk, then went with her to Mair Lougher's flat to see what was up. They let themselves in – Mrs Cuthbert had a key – and moved through the gloom of the little flat cautiously, calling Mair's name, asking if she was all right. In the sitting room the furniture was scattered, and they saw smears of blood on the carpet. The women went no further. Mrs Cuthbert ran to a flat on the top floor occupied by Mr Howells, yelling to him incoherently about Mair. He followed her downstairs and found Mrs Williams outside Mair's flat. She, too, was distraught.

Mr Howells went into the flat. He walked through the sitting room to the bedroom, then to the bathroom. Mair Lougher was lying in the bath. She was on her side, still clothed, her head resting on the wall by the tap unit. Her long hair obscured most of her face, and her clothes, hands and legs were covered with blood. She was perfectly still and no sound came from her. Mr Howells went outside and told the ladies Mair Lougher was dead. He went back inside, stepped into the bathroom and saw Mair's head move.

When DS Williams arrived at the flats to speak to Mrs Bennett she wasn't in. Walking back to his car, he heard someone call to him. It was Mrs Bennett, coming from the direction of Mair Lougher's flat, where she had gone after she heard something was wrong. She told DS Williams what Mr Howells had found; the detective rushed to the flat and saw Mair in the bath. She was making feeble movements with her hands on the tiles and on the sides of the bath. Williams radioed for an ambulance.

At that moment DC Paul James had just arrived at the complex. He was outside Enid Poole's flat when he heard a commotion from across the lawns. He could see that something was happening and went across to find out what it was. People stood back from the door of Mair Lougher's flat to let him go in. The scene inside was terrible – clothes and broken furniture thrown about the sitting room, the telephone torn out, blood on the walls, carpet and chairs. DC James found DS Williams in the bathroom, talking soothingly to a horrifically injured old lady lying slumped in the bath.

'Seeing Miss Lougher was a sight that I'd never experienced before and hopefully will never experience again,' DC James said. 'But it is something that you do have to put to the back of your mind, and carry on with the job in hand. Perhaps that gives you more impetus then to catch the man responsible.'

When the ambulance arrived, paramedic Richard Harris took a long time lifting Mair out of the bath, checking for signs of fractures or dislocations as he raised her, alert for any sudden crisis she might suffer. Harris noted she had serious head wounds and he believed, from the amount of congealed blood on her hair and clothes, that she had lain there for a long time. When a support collar had been strapped to her neck, Mair was taken to the ambulance and rushed to Cardiff Royal Infirmary.

'Immediately, my thoughts were of the huge implication we now had,' said DC James, 'with Mrs Poole being found the previous evening and now Miss Lougher found the following day. This meant we had two elderly ladies who had been attacked in their own homes, both of whom were very, very severely injured, and both of whom may die.'

As soon as the ambulance had taken Mair Lougher off to the infirmary, DS Williams went to talk to Mrs Bennett, the woman he had come to see in the first place. Rhona Bennett was eighty-one. Her flat was midway between Enid Poole's and Mair Lougher's, and she could see both flats from her sitting room window. She told DS Williams that at approximately 3.30 p.m. the previous day her door bell rang. She opened the door and saw a pleasant-looking, dark-haired young man wearing a black leather bomber jacket. He smiled and asked if his keys had been dropped though her letterbox. She said they hadn't, whereupon he looked confused and said he had been told the keys were left at the first flat. Mrs Bennett suggested he try the Davidsons' flat opposite – she knew they were in because she could see Gordon Davidson's umbrella in the stand outside. The young man thanked her and crossed to the other flat, where he pretended to ring the door bell. Mrs Bennett knew he was pretending because the bell was a loud one but she heard nothing. He waited a few seconds then came back to Mrs Bennett and said he had been told the keys would be at an elderly woman's flat at the end of the drive. That could as easily have meant Enid Poole's flat. Mrs Bennett showed the young man where it was. He thanked her and said, 'Sorry to bother you.'

When he walked off toward Mrs Poole's place, Mrs Bennett watched him from her window. She kept on watching until he turned the corner to Enid Poole's front door. Her uneasiness about the caller began to grow. She went across to the Davidsons' flat and told them what had happened. She was describing the caller when a young man walked past from the direction of Enid Poole's flat.

'Is that him?' Mr Davidson asked.

Mrs Bennett said it was. They watched until the stranger was out of sight again. They didn't see him after that.

It was obvious to DS Williams as he listened to Mrs Bennett's story that she felt guilty about having directed the man to Enid Poole's flat. Without mentioning that, DS Williams tried to make her feel better by pointing out how valuable it was to have good clear witness accounts such as hers.

At that point in the investigation and for some time afterwards, DS Williams had his own measure of distress to contend with. It troubled him to know that Mair Lougher had lain gravely injured in her bath for seventeen hours. He was a rational man and realized that nobody could have known what had happened, but nevertheless he felt terrible she hadn't been found. What disturbed him even more was that the attacker had not only beaten Enid and Mair, but he had torn out their telephones and locked them in, and for some time

Williams was dogged by the image of helplessness he saw when he walked into that bathroom.

'You can prepare as best you can,' he said, 'but the sight of some-one as small, as elderly as Mair trying to pull herself up out of the bath, and she couldn't... It's a sad thing to see.'

As soon as Mair Lougher arrived at Cardiff Royal Infirmary, a thorough evaluation of her injuries was carried out in A&E. The doctors estimated from the depth and other characteristics of her head and facial injuries that they were mostly heavy-impact wounds, caused by a wooden or metal weapon. Mair also had black eyes caused by punching; skull X-rays showed one fractured eye socket and fractures to other facial bones. Mair was admitted to a ward while arrangements were made for emergency surgery. She was visited there by her niece, Emma Wallace, who was understandably shocked at the first sight of her aunt. After an initially confusing exchange, the old lady recognized Emma and tried to speak to her. Her voice was unclear, a hoarse whisper. DC Jon Venners, one of the investigating team, was standing nearby. He stepped closer, anxious to hear anything that would help the investigation. Emma leaned down over the bed, putting her ear close to her aunt's mouth. Mair spoke again. Emma nodded and patted her hand.

'She's concerned about the woman who goes to the flat and does her hair,' Emma told the detective. 'She wants me to tell her she can't keep today's appointment.'

Later that day Mair was taken to theatre to have surgery on her fractured eye socket, a fractured cheekbone and two fractures on her jaw. When surgery was over, Mair was taken to a private room in a quiet part of the infirmary.

Door-to-door interviews, plus one voluntary statement made at Barry Police Station, established that the pleasant-looking stranger with the black bomber jacket had made calls on several elderly people on the afternoon of 20 March. At one o'clock 84-year-old Mrs

Charlotte Pritchard was at her home on The Parade, Barry, talking with her friend and neighbour, Maisie Henderson. Charlotte heard the front door bell ring; she answered it and saw a man of about thirty who fitted the description given to DS Williams by Mrs Bennett. He asked Mrs Pritchard if she knew the whereabouts of another woman; Mrs Pritchard had never heard of her, and by the time she spoke to the police she had forgotten the name the caller had used. He said that this other person was his aunt, a pensioner who had lived in the area for eighteen months. When Mrs Pritchard told him she was sorry but she didn't know the lady, the man then asked if he could use her telephone directory. Mrs Pritchard, innately alert to devious behaviour, became suspicious. She picked up the directory from the hall table and handed it to the caller, keeping him outside the door. She noticed that he took a quick look into the sitting room, then he riffled through the directory, made a show of finding what he was looking for, then left quickly, probably because he had seen that Mrs Pritchard was not alone.

At approximately 1.30 p.m. a man called at the home of Mrs Julia Morgan, a widow of seventy-five who lived at Sealyham Flats at Cross Howells in Barry, a five-minute walk away from Mrs Pritchard's home. This was another complex of flats occupied mainly by elderly people. Mrs Morgan was watching television when her intercom buzzed. She answered it and heard a man say he was looking for a Mrs George who lived at the flat next door. Mrs Morgan told him she remembered a *Miss* George who had lived in the next-door flat but was now in a home for the elderly. The visitor asked if Mrs Morgan would mind writing down the name of the nursing home for him. She said she would be glad to, and buzzed the caller in through the main entrance. When she answered his knock she saw a smiling, dark-haired man wearing a black leather jacket. He told Mrs Morgan that his name was Stephen and that he was Miss George's nephew. He took the piece of paper with the name of the nursing home written on it, then asked Mrs Morgan if he could have a drink of water – 'I've got a tickle in my throat; it feels just like a feather.'

Mrs Morgan told him to wait; she would get him a drink. She pulled the door to but didn't shut it completely. When she came out of the kitchen with the glass of water, the man was no longer out on the landing – he was inside the flat, standing near the door. This startled her. The man took the water, thanked her and drank it. He handed back the glass and asked if he could use the telephone: 'I'll reverse the charges, of course.' Mrs Morgan felt uneasy because the phone was in the lounge, but he smiled again warmly and she found herself agreeing. As they went to the lounge, she thought about Miss George and realized the old woman had no nephew, or any other relatives for that matter. The man was lying. She watched him dial a number. He listened for a moment, then said it was engaged and put down the receiver. He asked if he could have another glass of water. Mrs Morgan went to get it, wishing she had never let him in. Speaking to the police afterwards, her only explanation for allowing this situation to develop was that the man was confident, smart and likeable, and although she was uneasy she felt it was all right to comply with what he asked.

When she brought him his second glass of water he asked if her phone had a redial facility. She said it hadn't, and he appeared to drop the idea of calling anyone. Instead, he engaged Mrs Morgan in fairly one-sided conversation, which lasted for about fifteen minutes. During that time he told her again that his name was Stephen and that he had lived in Cheltenham and Worcestershire. He also said the last time he had visited Barry the lake outside Sealyham Flats had a number of tractors round it. He then lit a cigarette – without asking if he might – and used the phone again. There was no reply, he said, putting down the receiver.

When he asked for another glass of water, Mrs Morgan felt she really must get rid of him. She told him to go to the kitchen and help himself. She walked along the hallway a few steps behind him, thereby getting him out of the lounge and up nearer the front door – after which, she hoped, he would leave without her having to tell him bluntly to go. When he had gulped down his third glass of water he did leave, although that was after Mrs Morgan had said she was expecting guests.

The following day Mrs Morgan discovered that her caller had gone through her handbag, and he had taken some business cards, a Tesco receipt, and a few stamps from her purse. The police believed he stole those items because he either couldn't see what he was taking, or he got flustered and decided it was quicker to pocket the stuff than put it back.

At 3.20 that afternoon, Mrs Tanya Quilter returned to her flat at St Nicholas Road, around the corner from the complex where Enid Poole and Mair Lougher lived. A dark-haired man in a black leather jacket was standing in her porch. His hand was on the handle of her front door.

'Who are you?' Mrs Quilter demanded.

'I've been knocking on the door,' he said. 'How many people live here? I can't get an answer.'

Mrs Quilter ignored the question. 'What are you doing?'

He said he had lost his keys, possibly at the bus stop just outside the flat. He thought someone may have handed them in. Mrs Quilter told him she hadn't seen any keys.

'Sorry to trouble you,' he said, and walked away, leaving Mrs Quilter confused, but with a strong impression of how well mannered he was.

Mrs Quilter's husband, who had been in the flat all the time, heard no one knock on the door. Later, Mrs Quilter noticed that her lace curtains in the hallway had been disturbed, and payment cards on the windowsill had been moved.

The police estimated that Enid Poole had been attacked in her flat at 3.35 p.m., and twenty-five minutes later Linda Holt left her flat in the same complex to visit her friend, Emily Cuthbert, who lived directly opposite Mair Lougher. As Mrs Holt approached her friend's block she saw a man walking towards another entrance; she recalled he wore dark clothing. She carried on into the block and up two flights of stairs to the first floor. Opposite Mrs Cuthbert's flat she saw Mair Lougher outside her own front door, putting her key in the lock. The two women knew each other and they spoke briefly, then Mair said, 'I haven't got my hearing aid in. I'll give you a ring later.' Mrs Holt said that would be fine, and as she turned to Mrs Cuthbert's door she noticed the man she had seen earlier. He was coming down the stairs from the second floor. She glimpsed him one more time as Mrs Cuthbert let her in. This time he seemed to be hesitating on the landing.

The police believed the attacker had been doing just as Mrs Holt thought – hanging back on the landing between the two floors, waiting for her to go inside. He would have seen Mair Lougher returning from her Wednesday Club and pause to talk to Linda Holt. He probably grabbed Mair as she made to go inside, or he may have forced her into the flat, shutting the door behind them. The evidence showed that the attack had taken place close to the front door, so it could have been immediately after the door closed – the man wouldn't have wanted to be seen on the doorstep. It was also possible that because of Mair's small size and childlike weight he may simply have picked her up and forced her inside.

At 4.15 p.m. Mrs Gail Walters, the manageress of a local hotel, had just come home from work. She was in her ground-floor flat a few doors away from Enid Poole's. Gail was looking out of her window when she saw a man in a black leather bomber jacket walk past in the direction of Elm Tree Court, which was the escape route the attacker would have taken from Mair Lougher's flat. At the time Gail was not suspicious of the man.

While police were assembling an increasingly detailed picture of the attacker's movements on the day of the assaults, technicians from the forensic laboratory at Chepstow were examining the scenes of crime, which now numbered four: the flats of Enid Poole, Mair Lougher, Mrs Morgan and Mrs Quilter. A drop of blood was found on the wall of the landing outside Enid Poole's flat, and a fingerprint was lifted from the inside of a Charles and Diana biscuit tin on a shelf in Enid's kitchen. Fingerprints were taken from the homes of Mrs Morgan and Mrs Quilter. It was found subsequently that the blood was not a type-match for either Enid or Mair.

From 3 to 4 p.m. on Thursday, the day following the attacks, a meeting of all officers, uniformed and CID, was held at the Barry incident room. Detective Superintendent Wynne Phillips, heading the enquiry, brought everyone up to date on the investigative intelligence already to hand. They now knew that a Nationwide Building Society passbook, two purses, £150 in cash and three keys on a fob had been taken from Miss Lougher's flat. One of the keys had been used to lock the door when the attacker left.

An intriguing piece of intelligence was that on 20 March at 6.09 p.m., somebody tried to draw £200 from the cash machine at the Co-op Bank in The Hayes, Cardiff, using Enid Poole's Barclays Connect card; at 6.10 p.m. the thief tried again, twice; another two attempts were logged at 6.11 p.m. No money was paid out, but the cash machine failed to retain the card as it should have done after three failed attempts with a PIN. The police assumed that the person using the card was Enid Poole's attacker, and that he must have somehow obtained a number from Mrs Poole. Either she gave him the wrong one or he forgot it. Tape from CCTV cameras had been studied but showed nothing. The only possible witness was a schoolgirl who described a man she saw at the machine; she remembered a leather jacket and dark hair, but she didn't think she would be able to recognize his face if she saw him again. Detectives were cautiously presuming that the attacker had been travelling by train: the flats complex was a stone's throw from Barry railway station, and the Co-op Bank cash machine was just as close to Cardiff railway station.

Blood had been found on a lavatory door at Barry station, but it had been exposed to too much contamination and was useless for testing. That was disappointing. Blood was now a factor in the investigation because the blood of an unknown person had been found near Enid Poole's flat, so there was speculation that her attacker had been injured at the time he assaulted her. If unexplained blood turned up in a context even remotely connected with the current investigation, it would be grouped, and where possible it would also be submitted to DNA analysis.

A final item of information was that photofit pictures had been prepared from descriptions given by women who recollected what the attacker looked like; of these, Mrs Bennett was very happy with hers and gave it better than eight out of ten for resemblance. That particular picture would be used on media appeals.

When the meeting was over, DI Kevin O'Neill toured Barry in a squad car with a loudspeaker on top, urging people to make sure their elderly relatives and neighbours were safe and well.

On the morning of Monday 25 March an arrest was made, but it came to nothing. A local man had been anonymously reported, but his alibi for the day of the attacks was solid. Blood found on his leather jacket turned out to be his own.

Two days later the police conducted reconstruction exercises, stop-checking people near the flats complex and at the Co-op Bank at The Hayes. HTV West ran an appeal on the programme *Regional Crimestoppers* on 1 April, and would run it daily for a week. On 4 April Mrs Bennett's photofit picture, superimposed on a photograph of a police officer wearing clothes similar to the attacker's, was released to the press. It was also issued as a flier with the heading HELP US CATCH THIS MAN BEFORE HE STRIKES AGAIN. When nearly a week had passed without any further significant progress,

Detective Superintendent Wynne Phillips decided to widen the search beyond the locality and approached the *Crimewatch* team about the possibility of airing an appeal.

There was no doubt that the flow of evidence was diminishing. But that was inevitable, as DS Williams pointed out. 'As time goes on, it tends to become more difficult because people have helped all they can, they've told you what they know, and with the passage of time the useful information becomes less and less.'

About this time, DC James brought together Enid Poole's relatives, the Mounters, and Mair Lougher's niece, Emma Wallace. They met in a waiting room at Cardiff Royal Infirmary. Over tea, DC James told them there was no news yet of the attacker, but he needed to sound them out on something: the police wanted to go public with photographs showing Enid's and Mair's injuries. What did the relatives feel about that?

Emma wasn't sure. She didn't think her aunt would like it.

DC James understood, but he stressed that the idea was to bring home to people the appalling viciousness of what this man had done.

Sheila Mounter asked DC James if he really thought it would help. He said he did. The relatives thought about it a little longer, then they told him to go ahead. Within days, the terrible pictures of the battered old ladies were hanging in police stations, on public notice boards, in railway station buffets and on the front pages of newspapers. The public responded with shock and near disbelief. The photographs woke consciences and stimulated anger, and they put more pressure on the police to find the man who could do such things to frail, innocent people. Emma Wallace, for one, was glad she had agreed to the photographs being used.

'They helped a lot,' she said, 'because I'm sure that people were so disgusted as to what had happened that everybody, I think, felt that they wanted to catch the person who had done this horrific act.'

Given the public reaction, DS Phil Williams had no misgivings about the pictures either. 'I don't think words could have conveyed what actually happened then. And yes, we did think about the consequences of showing those photographs, but our view was: let people see what's happening.'

On the afternoon of 11 April a distraction burglar, using a similar MO to the man being hunted in Barry, struck at the home of an elderly woman in Rumney, a suburb of Cardiff. Mrs Parsons, who was eighty-six, opened her door to a man who asked if he could speak to a Mr Perkins. When Mrs Parsons told him that no Mr Perkins lived at that address, and that she didn't know any Mr Perkins, the man asked for a telephone directory and a glass of water. Mrs Parsons had just come home after a spell in hospital; she had also been celebrating her birthday that day, so she was not as alert as she would normally have been. Later, when her visitor had gone, she discovered that £5 was missing from her purse. The man, as Mrs Parsons recalled, was quite young, with dark hair and a pleasant manner. He wore a black leather jacket.

Two days later, Rick Holden, a clinical psychologist and former police officer, produced a report setting out a likely profile of the man the Barry police were after. Holden believed the offender would have previous convictions with dishonesty and disorder offences among them, and that he was likely to have tried to use the Connect card on his way home.

Crimewatch transmitted a reconstruction of the attacks on Enid and Mair on Thursday 25 April. The viewer response was good, with a total of 200 calls to the studio and incident room. A number of names of possible suspects were put forward, and they would all be followed up. Eric Williams, an off-duty detective sergeant in Worcester, saw the appeal and believed the style and physical description of the wanted man could have been a character sketch of a Welshman he'd had in custody back in 1994.

After the programme Eric thought some more about it, remembering the witnesses' descriptions, the re-enactment, the offender's potential for offhanded violence; the more he thought about it, the more he was convinced that the *Crimewatch* appeal had resurrected a nasty customer from his past. The name of the man escaped him for the moment, but not the circumstances. On a Saturday afternoon in February 1994, Eric had been on duty as a uniform custody sergeant at Worcester Police Station. Around tea time, two CID officers brought in the Welshman and one other man, both having been arrested on suspicion of causing criminal damage. CID had been responding to a complaint call about two men causing a nuisance in the grounds of St Thomas Lodge at Tything, Worcester, a sheltered housing complex for elderly people. Both men were drunk, the caller had reported, and they were suspected of having damaged a window.

The detectives had no difficulty in finding the men. They searched them, and in the Welshman's pocket they found a wage envelope; there was a payslip inside with the name of a care worker at the complex printed on it. Door-to-door enquiries revealed that the Welshman had been telling residents he was a policeman, and that he had been chasing a convicted rapist he suspected of 'doing drugs' in the grounds of the complex. Eventually, the second man was eliminated from the complaint and released. When the Welshman was taken into custody, he became abusive to Eric Williams, calling him a 'fat English bastard' and other offensive names. Since the man appeared to be severely drunk, his rights were not read to him. When he started kicking the cell walls and door, he was told to take off his shoes, which brought on another torrent of offensive language. Later, when he had sobered up, the man appeared to have undergone a change of personality. Expressing himself civilly, he denied any wrongdoing at the old people's complex and maintained he had been following a convicted rapist. He had found the wage packet and picked it up – he had wanted to return it to whoever had dropped it.

There had been no cheque in the envelope when he found it, he said, though one was now missing.

He was eventually charged with burglary and criminal damage. He denied both charges and was bailed by Eric Williams. When he failed to appear at South Worcestershire Magistrates' Court on 29 April, a warrant was issued for his arrest, but Eric Williams had no recollection of him being apprehended.

On the day following the *Crimewatch* appeal, Eric Williams pulled the file on the 1994 Worcester case and looked up the name of the abusive Welshman: it was Leslie Stuart Salter. He then called the Barry incident room and spoke to DC Anzani-Jones, the HOLMES supervisor. Eric outlined the two-year-old burglary case and said it might be an idea at least to check up on this character, whom he had remembered mainly because he was distinctly 'dangerous'. He added that when Salter was sober, he drew no attention to himself. He was physically unmemorable and exuded a certain charm. However, the Worcester officers had been instinctively wary of Salter's potential f or violence.

Eric Williams's call to the incident room was noted, but was not treated with any special urgency. Leslie Salter's name went on the end of the list of people to be checked.

At this stage of the investigation Mair Lougher was making a good recovery in hospital. Day by day her strength improved, and she began to show signs of her old vigour. 'It wasn't until she'd had the surgery on her face that she felt a little bit better in herself,' said her niece Emma. 'Some of the bruising was looking better, shall we say... I think then she felt herself that she was looking better, and then feeling a bit better about everything.'

Enid Poole, on the other hand, had made no perceptible progress. She lay in her hospital bed and appeared increasingly to be turning inwards, avoiding an outside world that frightened her. 'As the weeks went by, her mental state wasn't getting any better,' said

Sheila Mounter. 'I wondered if she would make it... if her mental state would improve. But she was a very frightened lady, and the injuries to her head were very bad.'

Enid and Mair were strong individuals, Emma Wallace observed, and different things had happened to each of them. 'With Auntie Mair I think it was mostly the scarring on the face, whereas with Mrs Poole it was mentally entirely different.'

The hunt for the attacker, meanwhile, went on. It was 17 May when DS Williams ran a Police National Computer check on Leslie Salter and found he had appeared in court thirteen times since 1981 and had several convictions. The Police Archives Centre in Cardiff was able to supply more details of the offences, and an interesting detail came to light: in a case of distraction burglary, Salter had conned his way into the victim's home by asking for a glass of water. DS Williams had an immediate and strong feeling that this was the man they were looking for. He checked for local fingerprint records but was told they were held at Gwent. That afternoon he drove to Gwent and picked up copies of Salter's prints, which he then took to the Fingerprint Bureau in Cardiff. An officer there said he would check them against the prints from the scenes of crime at Barry and would phone through his findings to the Barry incident room.

Hours passed, but no call came. DS Williams finally rang the Fingerprint Bureau, anxious to know if he was on the right track. He was told there was a ninety per cent match with two prints found in Mrs Morgan's home at Sealyham Flats, and a partial match – nine rather than the required minimum sixteen points of individuality – with the print from the lid of the biscuit tin at Enid Poole's. The officer at the bureau promised DS Williams they would continue to work on this print in the hope of gaining a full identification.

The reaction in the incident room was jubilant. As DC James put it: 'There was great relief and happiness.' The team were aware they still had a lot to prove before there was a case, but now they knew who the villain was, so they were out of the dark.

Finding their man was the first new headache. Salter's last known address, recorded on a conviction sheet, was in Newport, in Gwent, but he didn't live there any more and there was no forwarding address. He had no driving licence, he did not claim government benefits, and he paid no income tax. It takes a unique talent to slide through the system without tags and numbers, but Leslie Salter appeared to have done it. A search of the records happened to turn up his brother's address. DS Williams went to see him and hit another dead end: Leslie hadn't been in touch for a long time, the brother said, and the family had no idea where he lived – he had been giving them false addresses for years.

On Monday 20 May, through a network of contacts, DS Williams finally managed to get an address. If the information was correct, Salter was living in the Roath district of Cardiff. The enquiry team held a meeting in Detective Superintendent Phillips' office to decide on a strategy for securing an arrest.

Elsewhere that afternoon, at Gower Road in Risca, Gwent, eighty-year-old Mrs Doreen Hulton was at home alone when she answered the door to a man fitting Salter's description. He held up a bunch of keys, which he said he'd found on the drive.

'Are they yours?' he asked.

Mrs Hulton said they weren't, but they could belong to her cousin, who had been there earlier. 'If you wait a minute I'll ring her.'

She called her cousin's number, but the line was engaged. She invited the man inside to wait until she tried again. He sat down and quickly engaged Mrs Hulton in conversation.

He told her he had been thinking about buying a house like hers to share with his two daughters. Would Mrs Hulton mind if he looked upstairs? His request flustered her; she said no, she didn't want him doing that. But he went upstairs anyway. He stayed up there for about five minutes and came down only when Mrs Hulton called out and told him she didn't want him up there.

He asked for a pen and paper. Mrs Hulton shook her head, nervous now and frightened. She asked the man to leave. He nodded and opened the door. 'You should be careful who you let in your house,' he said, smiling as he left.

When Mrs Hulton went upstairs she discovered that her wardrobe had been searched, but nothing had been taken.

About half an hour later a man called at the home of 87-year-old Emma Jenkins at Fielding Terrace, Pontymister. He showed her some keys and asked her if she had lost them. Mrs Jenkins said they weren't hers, then she called over her shoulder, asking if anybody had lost a bunch of keys. Several visitors' voices called back – no, they hadn't lost any. The man left without another word.

Roughly twenty minutes later a pleasant-mannered young man called at the nearby home of Austin Brent, seventy-one, and dangled a bunch of keys in front of him.

'Would these be yours at all?'

Mr Brent said they weren't his.

'Pardon me asking,' the caller said, 'but are you disabled?'

'No, not at all. But Mrs Weaver is.'

Mr Brent then directed the man to Mrs Weaver's house. Later, Mr Brent would explain that he thought the caller was looking for a disabled person because he knew, some way or another, that a disabled person owned the keys.

When the dark-haired man knocked on Mrs Weaver's door a few minutes later he made no mention of keys, and his manner was noticeably brusque.

'Mrs Weaver?'

'That's right, yes.'

'I'm from the council rent department. I need to speak to you about an urgent matter.'

Megan Weaver, who was eighty-six and quite infirm, invited him into her living room, where he told her that arrears of rent had accumulated to a point where she must take action and clear her debt to the council. He then shocked her by saying that the back rent was £800. She had never owed anyone so much money in her entire life.

'But you have got it, haven't you?'

'At the bank,' she told him.

He said the debt had to be paid that day, in cash, otherwise she would be prosecuted. If she put on her coat, he would take her to the bank to draw the money. Flustered, Mrs Weaver did as he said. As she moved about in the passageway getting her scarf and coat the man kept hurrying her, telling her they had to get into the town centre before the bank closed.

'And don't forget your chequebook, love.'

When they got outside, Mrs Weaver was surprised to find he had no car. It was raining, and she pulled her scarf up over her head. They would catch a bus, the man said, but it was hard for Mrs Weaver to walk any distance because of her crippling arthritis. When she had hobbled a few steps the man picked her up and carried her to the bus stop.

When eventually they got to the bank, it had just closed. The man told Mrs Weaver to ring the bell. She did, and because she was obviously distressed and frail-looking, and they had only just closed anyway, the cashier unlocked the door and let Mrs Weaver in. The man waited outside.

After a couple of minutes Mrs Weaver came to the door and beckoned the man. There was only £600 in her account, she said. She had more at the Halifax, but they would be closed by now. The man went into the bank with her, telling her to take her time and calling her 'Nan' loud enough for the staff to hear. He explained to the cashier in a low voice that the old lady had just got out of hospital and that he had been paying her rent while she was away. He told Mrs Weaver to draw the £600; it would do for the moment. When she was given the cash he held out his hand: 'Let me have that for safe keeping.' He also took her chequebook and house keys.

Out on the street again, they walked slowly to the bus stop. As a bus approached, the man hurried ahead of Mrs Weaver and jumped on. She couldn't make it to the stop before the bus pulled away. The man waved to her as he went past.

At approximately the time the young man was telling Mrs Weaver to ring the bell at the bank, three unmarked police cars were drawing up at different positions to the front and rear of the house at Stone Road in Roath, Cardiff, where informants said Leslie Salter now lived. Possible escape routes were watched by officers in two of the cars while DS Williams and two other detectives went up the front steps. DS Williams knocked on the door and a young woman opened it. He introduced himself and told her his colleagues were DCs Wheeler and Jones.

'We need to talk to Leslie Salter.'

He wasn't back yet from work, the woman said. What was it about?

'Assaults on two elderly women in Barry in March of this year.'

The woman was visibly shocked. 'How does that concern Les?'

DS Williams asked if she'd mind if they came in and waited for Mr Salter. She looked reluctant. Williams smiled and promised they wouldn't be a nuisance. The woman hesitated, then she stood aside and let them file in.

In the house, DS Williams waited in the front room while DC Wheeler and DC Jones went to the back living room with the woman. During the time the detectives waited they learned that the woman was Salter's common-law wife, Denise, and that she and Salter – he was using his real name – lived there with her parents, who owned the property. Salter, who nowadays claimed to be a painter and decorator, had told Denise that he had been a police officer in Gwent but had been retired on grounds of ill health.

At 6.05 p.m. Salter let himself into the house with his own key. As he walked along the hallway, he called out, 'Denise, I'm home.' DS Williams followed him up the hall to the back living room. As soon as he opened the door all three officers seized him.

Salter was formally arrested for the robbery of Mair Lougher and Enid Poole at Barry, and for a burglary at Julia Morgan's home at Sealyham Flats. When DS Williams cautioned him, he said nothing. He was handcuffed and searched: the officers found he was carrying £638.14 in cash, a Midland Bank chequebook in the name of Mrs Megan Weaver, his house keys, another bunch of keys, and two keys on a fob bearing Mrs Weaver's name. Salter was taken to Fairwater Police Station at Cardiff.

DC James told the Mounters and Mair Lougher's niece, Emma Wallace, that an arrest had been made and that the police had no doubt he was the right man. The Mounters were pleased and relieved. Emma's reaction was a little different. She asked DC James not to tell her aunt just yet.

'My main worry was how Auntie Mair would take it,' said Emma, 'but even though I'd been quite strong, that was the day that I broke down.'

At Cardiff, Leslie Salter was closely questioned by DS Williams and DC Venners. Throughout questioning he stubbornly denied everything. The forensic evidence, he said, was wrong. As for his movements on 20 March, when Enid Poole and Mair Lougher were assaulted, he claimed he had been decorating the house of a Mrs Reilly all that day; he had gone out once, to B&Q in Pont Prennau, to buy some tongue-and-groove. He had no idea how a fingerprint with nine characteristics identical to his could have turned up on a biscuit tin at Mrs Poole's – it all had to be a police blunder.

While Salter was being questioned, officers in the Barry incident room made urgent enquiries about the chequebook. They soon discovered that the Mrs Weaver in question had been conned out of money in Risca on Monday 20 May by a man who had then abandoned her in the town centre. The incident was on record at Risca Police Station.

Wider-reaching fingerprint records were searched, revealing that Salter's prints had been found at the scenes of numerous other distraction burglaries. He went on denying all charges and told the police that the fingerprints were not his.

During a further session of questioning, on 23 May, DS Williams demolished Salter's claim that he had gone to B&Q on 20 March. Williams had discovered that the branch of B&Q at Pont Prennau had not opened to the public until the following week. Salter was visibly dumbfounded.

Meanwhile, new material was steadily being added to the case. On the morning of 21 May, the day after Salter was arrested, Ellen Prescott, seventy-five, of Risca, Gwent, noticed that the keys she normally kept on a hook in a cupboard near her front door were missing. She didn't report this to the police until the next day. Normally, when Mrs Prescott went out she locked her doors and left the keys in the porch, but she kept them in the cupboard when she was at home. She told the police she remembered leaving the keys in the cupboard on the previous Saturday.

Following the discovery that the keys were gone, Mrs Prescott then found that a tan purse containing £100 and some photographs was missing from a chest of drawers in her bedroom. She reported this new discovery to the police. The bunch of keys found on Salter when he was arrested were identified by Mrs Prescott as being hers. The police presumed that Salter took the keys when Mrs Prescott was at the laundry on 20 May; he entered the house, stole the purse, then left the house, taking the keys with him.

Later, the tan purse was found empty, floating in the cistern of the men's lavatory at the Risca Working Men's Club. Salter admitted drinking at the club on the afternoon of 20 May. Witnesses interviewed at the club said he had been passing himself off as a police officer. He had been seen going into the lavatory where the purse was found. This offence was added to the list of charges being lined up against Salter.

During a session of questioning on 23 May, DC James interrupted the interview and asked to speak to DS Williams outside. As soon as the door to the interview room was closed, DC James turned excitedly to his sergeant. He had just spoken to the Fingerprint Bureau in Cardiff, he said. They told him they had just redeveloped the fingerprint from Enid Poole's biscuit tin.

'They got a hit,' DC James said. 'The print is definitely Salter's. They made sixteen characteristics.'

The inadmissible had become admissible. Salter's presence in Enid Poole's flat had been proved.

'I knew he was finished,' DS Williams said later. 'His fingerprints were there, his DNA was there... Finally, he'd have to stand there and admit it was him.'

On 23 May, at 7.15 p.m., in the custody area at Fairwater Police Station, Leslie Stuart Salter was charged with robbery of, and grievous bodily harm with intent on, Enid Poole; he was additionally charged with robbery of, and grievous bodily harm with intent on, Mair Lougher. After appearing at Cardiff Court he was remanded in custody to Cardiff Prison.

Mair Lougher, almost completely recovered from her injuries, would soon be leaving hospital and going back home. Enid Poole, on the other hand, was languishing in a Barry nursing home, prey to spreading infections that she lacked the resources to fight. 'She was so frightened,' said Sheila Mounter. 'All she wanted to do was hold your hand – most of the time I was just reassuring her and being close to her.'

On 7 November, at Cardiff Crown Court, Salter pleaded guilty to nineteen offences, including robbery, wounding and burglary. Lord Justice Tucker sentenced him to four terms of life imprisonment. 'It is now time for the public to be protected from you for a very long time,' the judge said, adding the recommendation that Salter serve a minimum twelve years.

Exactly a month later, on 7 December, Enid Poole died at her nursing home in Barry having never recovered from her terrible ordeal. On the day of her funeral, DS Williams, DC James and DI O'Neill had a quiet drink after the service and discussed the possibility of bringing a murder charge against Salter. Enid Poole had died nine months after the attack, which shortened the chances of a conviction – but, as DS Williams pointed out, everyone knew it was the attack that had destroyed the quality of Enid's life and eventually killed her. Apart from a yearning to see justice done, the detectives felt a real threat of justice being thwarted: Salter was considering an appeal and was prepared to say he only pleaded guilty because his barrister told him to. There was also talk of him revamping his alibi, cutting out the part about going to B&Q. The detectives knew that if Salter did appeal there was always a chance he would get off, or at least have his sentence shortened.

As time passed, more thought was given to the possibility of a murder charge, and eventually it was decided that the police should consult the Crown Prosecution Service. They did, and the learned opinion of CPS lawyers was that with a properly prepared case they should stand a good chance of securing a conviction.

Before the case papers were prepared for submission to the CPS, the detectives thought it best to talk to Sheila and Richard Mounter to sound out their feelings about a murder charge. They were approached at the end of January 1997, and at first they were reluctant to retrace the whole painful territory. On the other hand, they had no doubt that Enid Poole had died as a result of the beating she took. 'As far as I'm concerned,' Richard said, 'with her health as it was at the time, there was no reason at all why she couldn't have gone on and got her centenary.'

Sheila agreed. 'Her life changed completely after that night. She'd been an outgoing, happy person, and overnight she became a shell of her former self.'

In the end the Mounters acknowledged the justice of the police action and gave it their support. 'He'd been given four life sentences, with a recommendation to serve a minimum of twelve years,' said Richard. 'We weren't sure whether going for a murder conviction would actually increase that sentence or not. But eventually we thought, well, he left them both to die in the first instance, so go for it.'

It was established, through interviews with people who knew Enid, that before the attack she had been an independent and alert woman who enjoyed an active social life. When the staff at her nursing home were interviewed, they all spoke of her quality of life as being very poor. Following the attack she had lost her freedom of movement, much of her speech, and all of her confidence. She constantly asked, 'Am I safe?'

Dr Stephen Jones, Mrs Poole's GP, made a statement to DC James saying he had known Enid for many years. He firmly believed that the fear she had experienced after the attack had led to her physical and mental decline, which rendered her unable to combat the infections that eventually killed her.

Dr Sastry, the geriatric consultant at Cardiff Royal Infirmary who attended Enid after her accident, said she was a fiercely independent lady whose frailty began with her injuries. After 20 March she began to deteriorate. It became quite clear to Dr Sastry and other professionals attending her that the beating was the cause of her deterioration – 'And hence,' Dr Sastry concluded, 'there was no other cause for her death.'

Police surgeon Dr Sally Wood signed a statement setting out in detail the injuries she found when she examined Enid Poole at Cardiff Royal Infirmary on 21 March 1996. Pathologist Iain West was shown a medical report by Sue Claydon, a Home Office pathologist who conducted a post-mortem on Enid Poole at the University Hospital of Wales; he agreed that the assault on Enid was a major contributing factor in her death.

In due course DC Paul James charged Salter in prison with the murder of Enid Poole. Salter's response was: 'I'm going to sue you if my photos get in the papers again.'

Salter clearly bore DC James a grudge, probably because James had taken statements from Salter's common-law wife, Denise, which appeared to confirm his alibi. The alibi was later proved to be a fabrication, so Denise faced possible prosecution for attempting to pervert the course of justice.

DC James had his own firm opinion of Salter, which he still holds. 'I think he's quite a clever character. I think that before committing his crimes he looks at the area and the type of people he wishes to prey on... I think he spends a lot of time in planning what he does, and I think he is quite an intelligent person. I felt that he deserved to be charged with Mrs Poole's murder, and I was glad to be there.'

On Thursday 15 January 1998, at Cardiff Crown Court, Leslie Stuart Salter, aged thirty-one, stood trial for the murder of Enid Poole. The medical evidence was compelling and again Salter's defence entered a guilty plea. The judge, Mr Justice Thomas, sentenced him to a further term of life imprisonment.

Afterwards, DS Phil Williams, speaking of Salter's viciousness towards Enid and Mair, said: 'He didn't need to do it to take their money, or anything else that they had. He did that because he wanted to. I don't know what his motivation was, but there was never a need for it, and I think that's what I'll remember about him.'

index

index